47 Patterns for Adult Coloring

by Linn Littlebelle

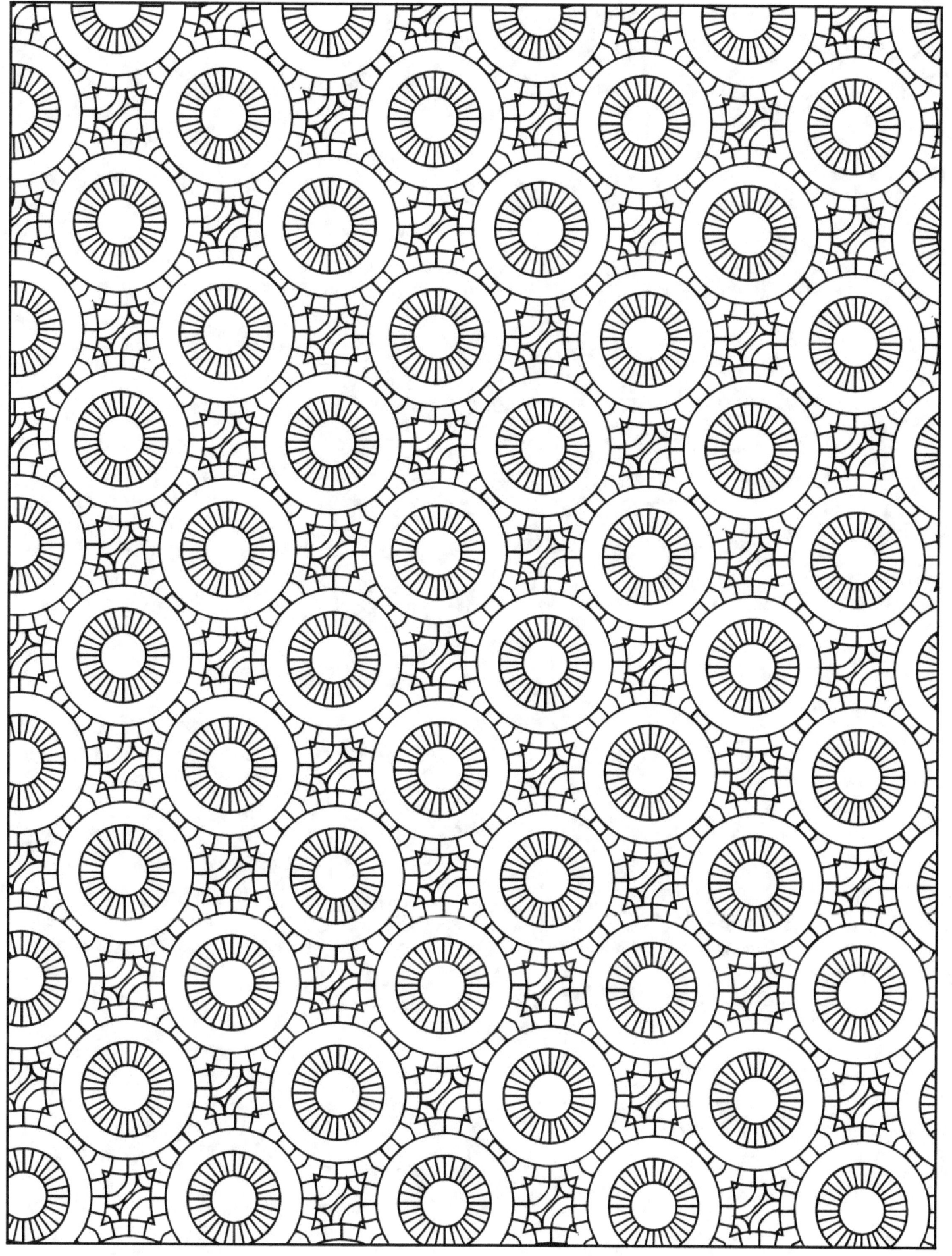

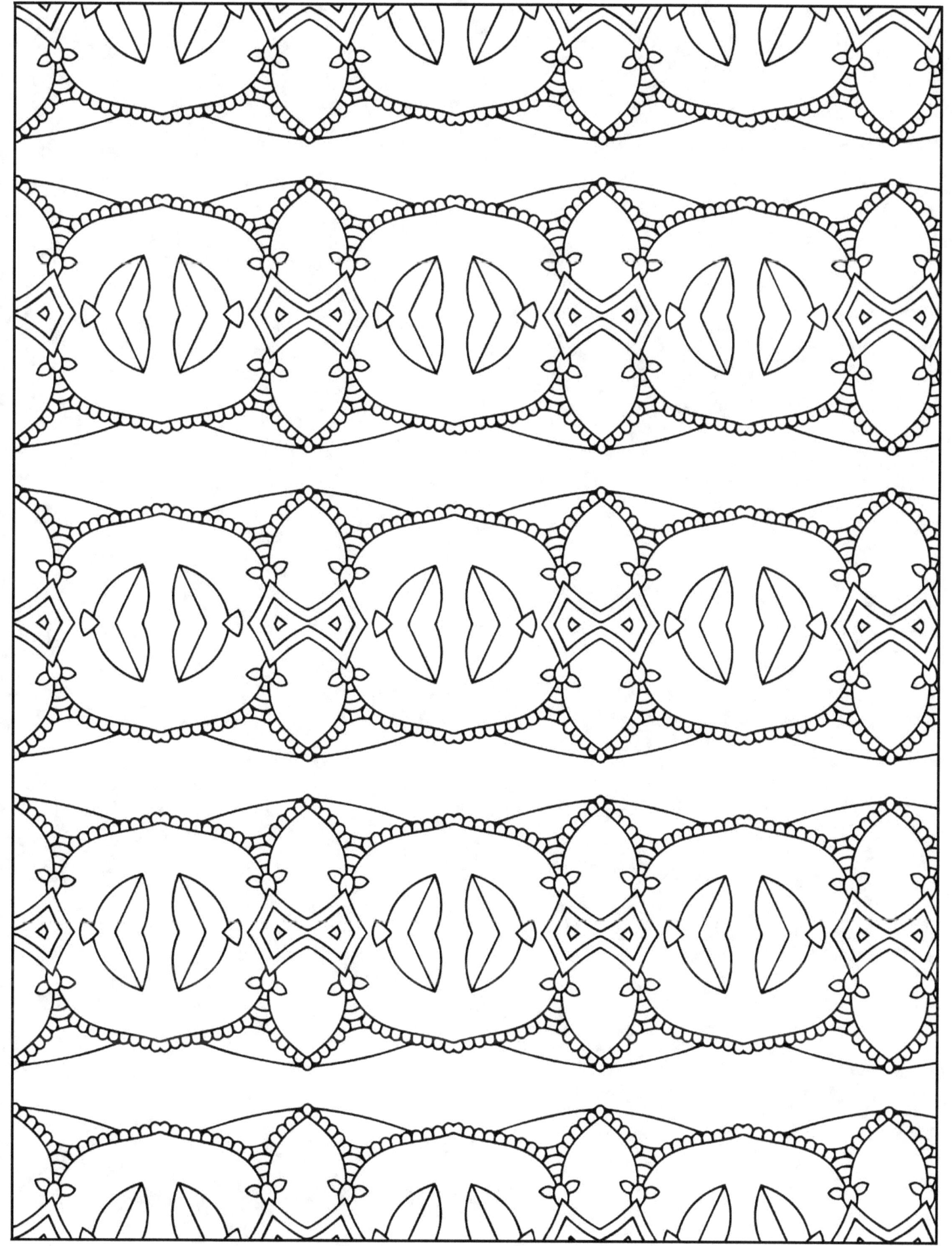

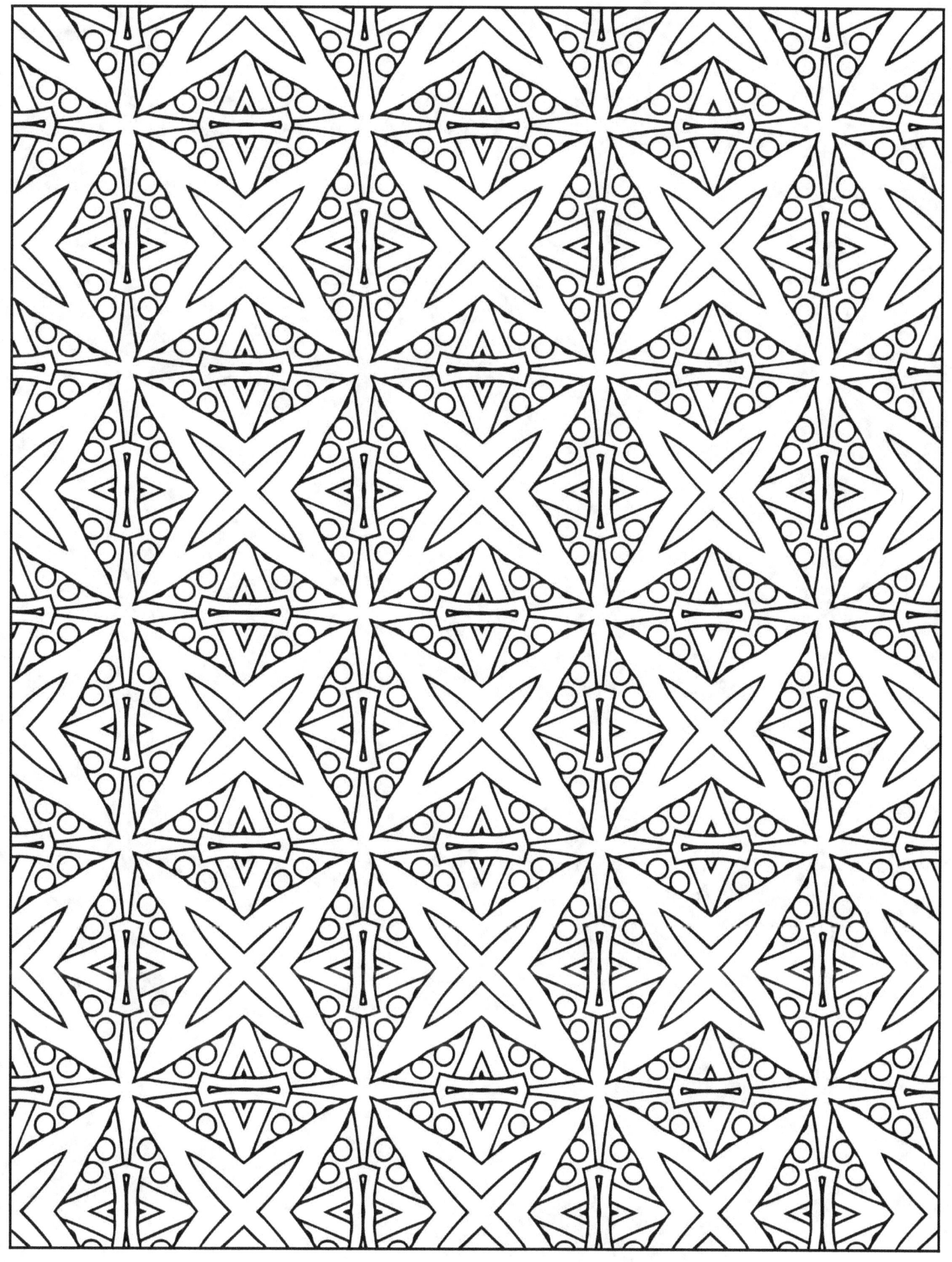

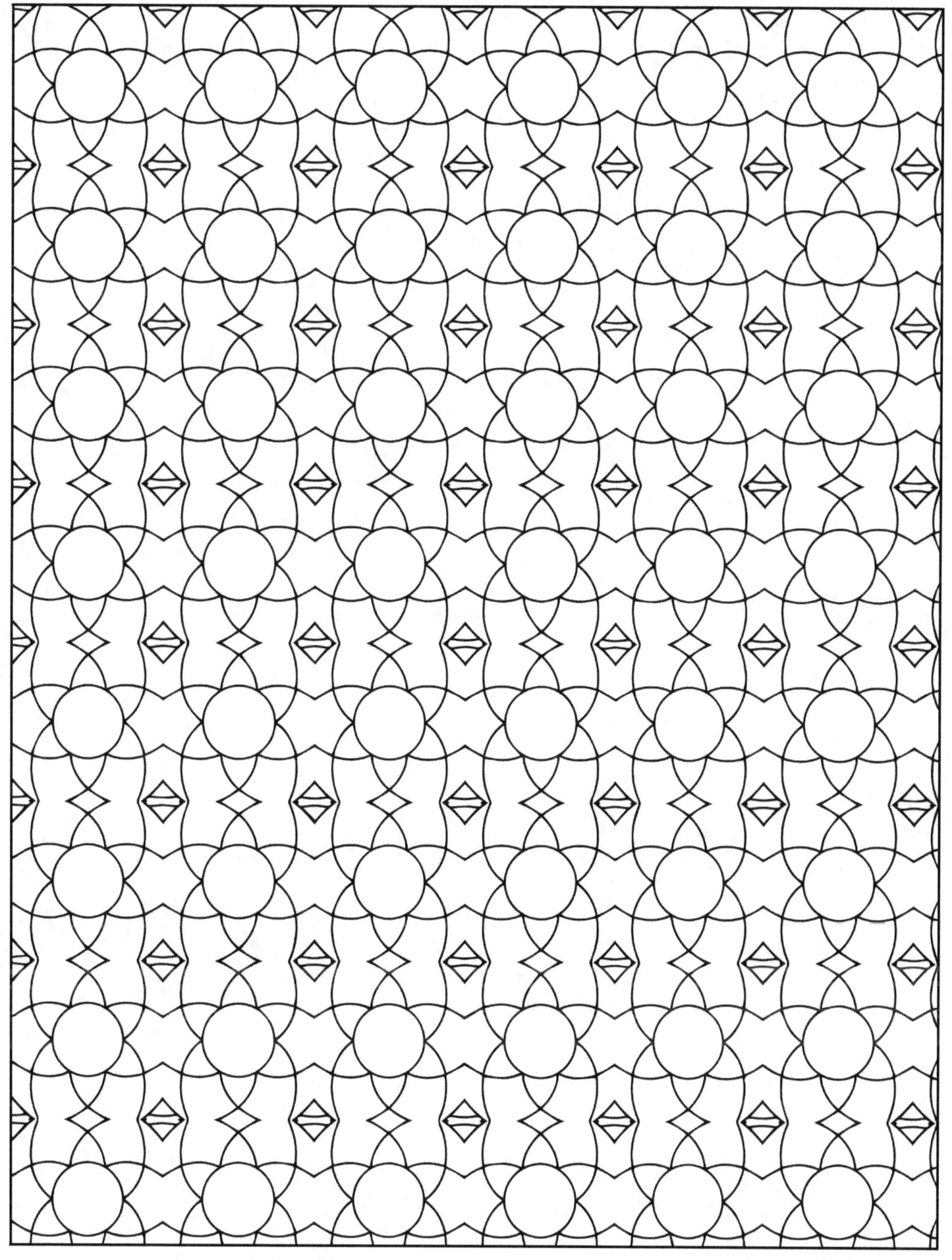

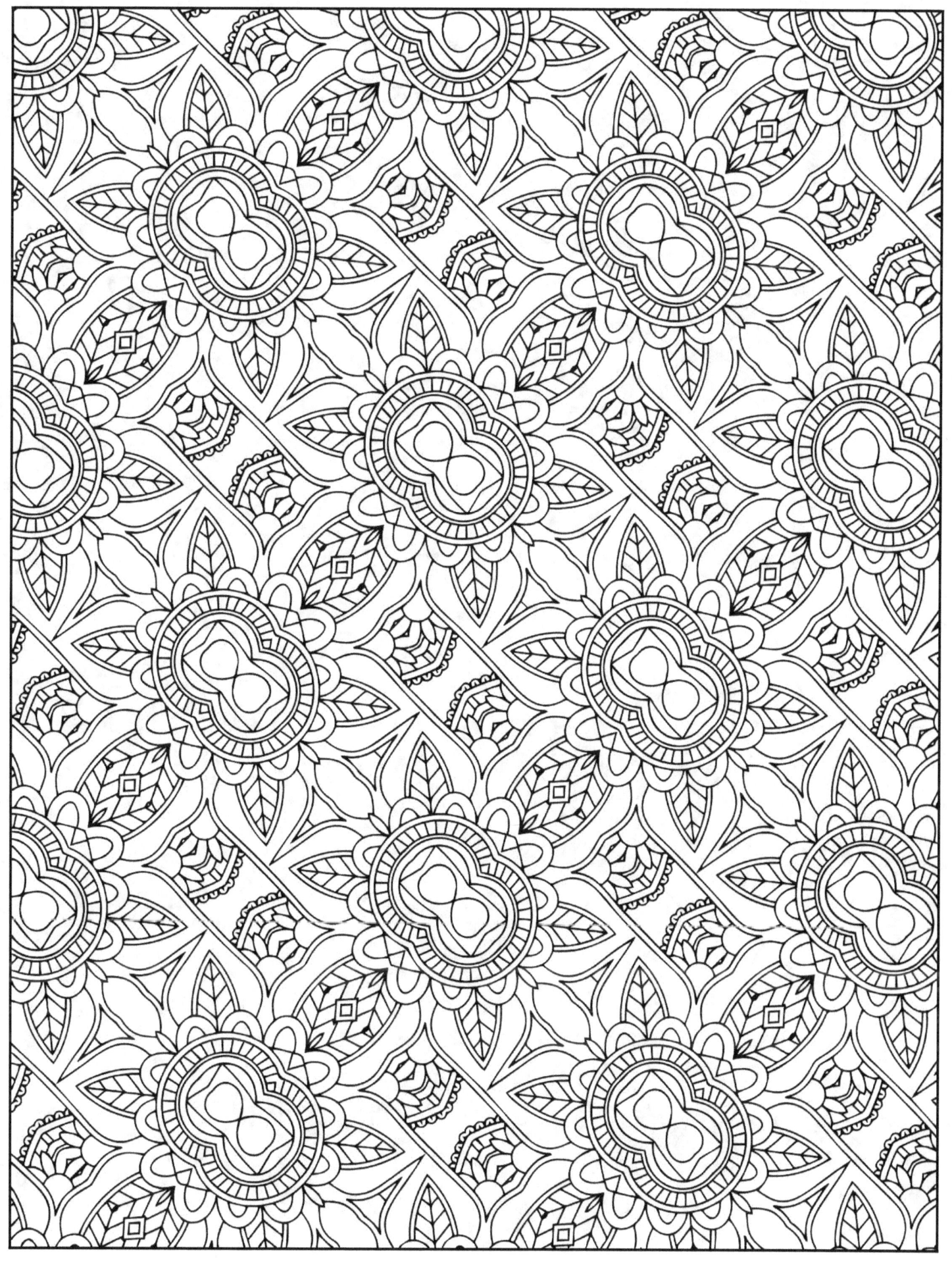

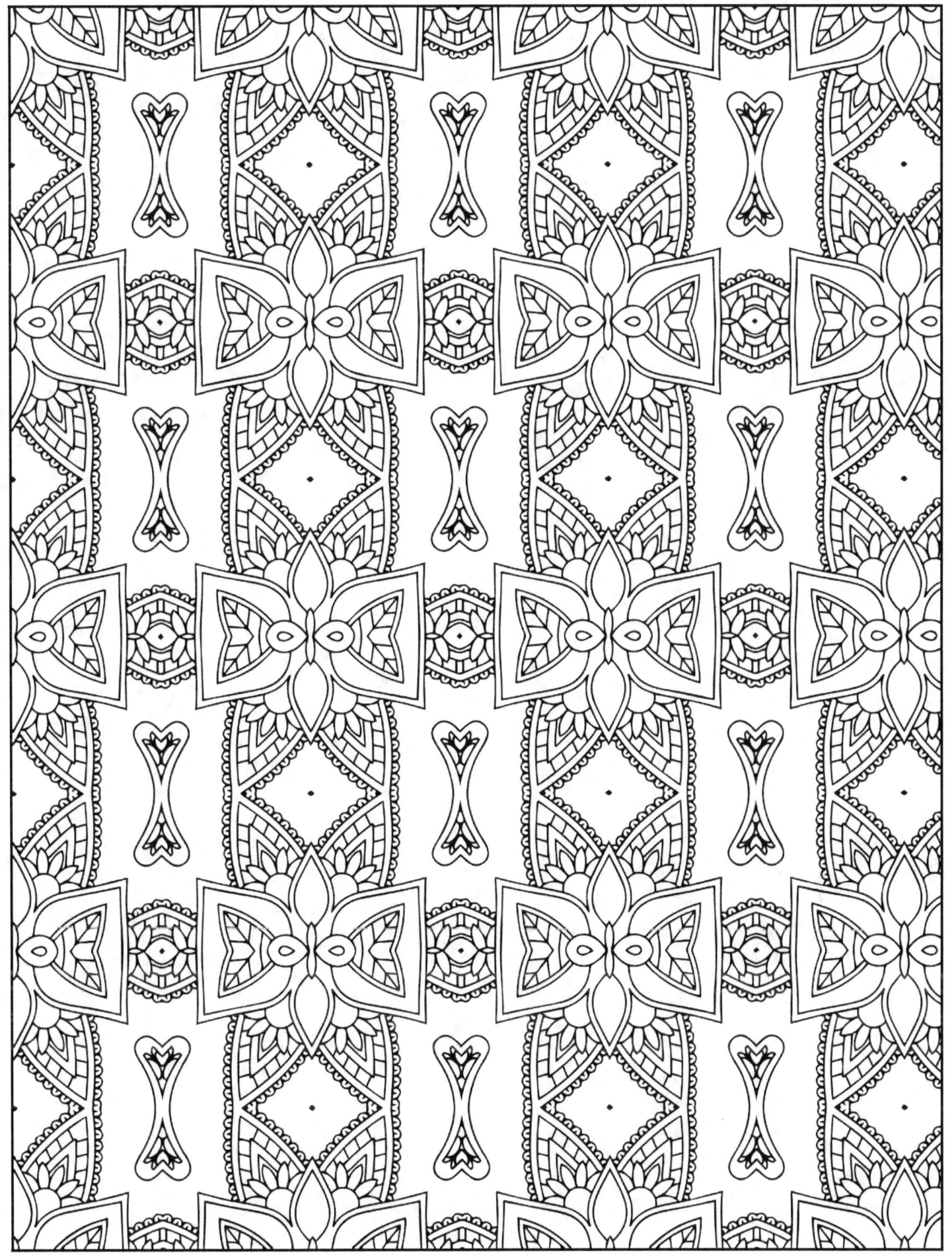

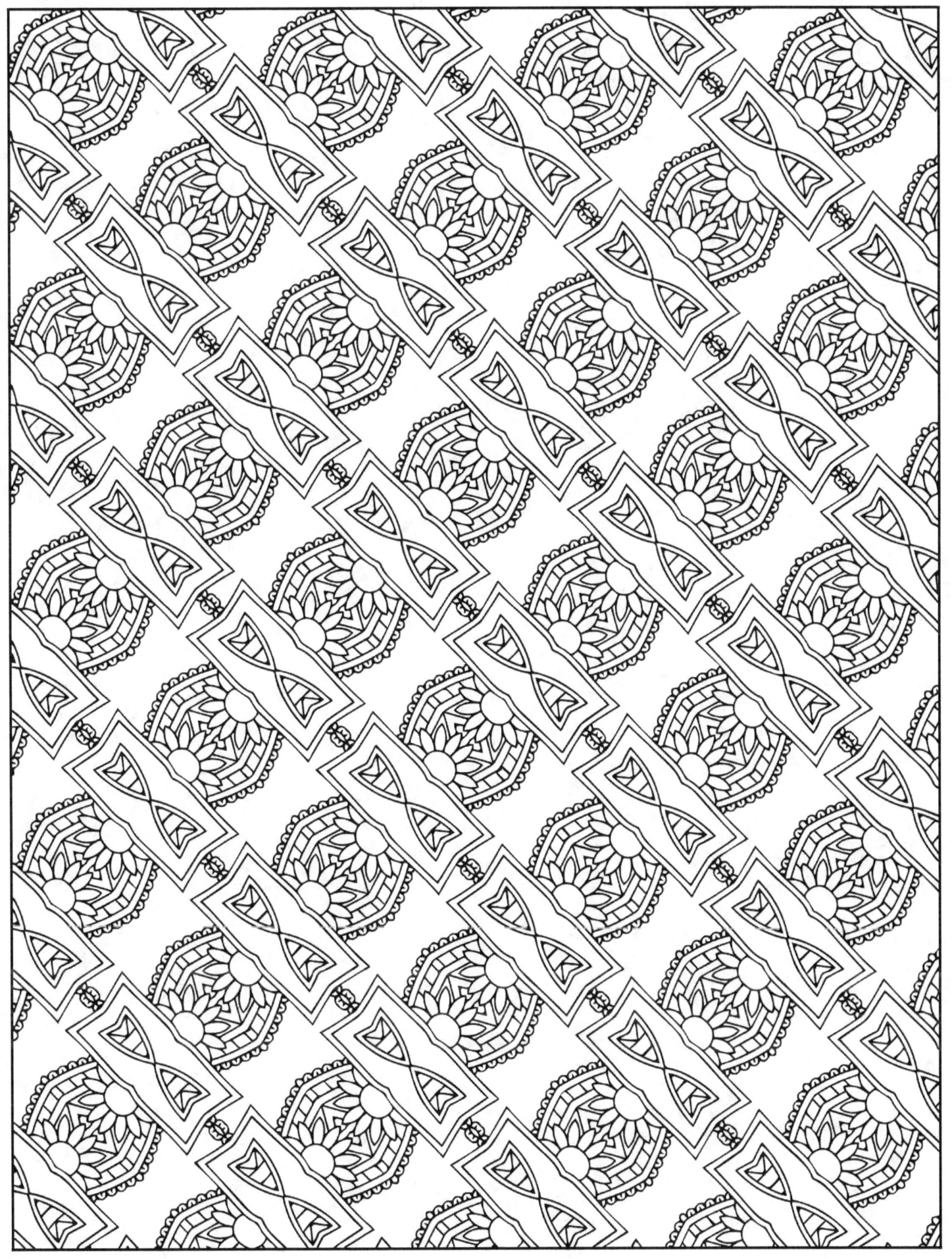

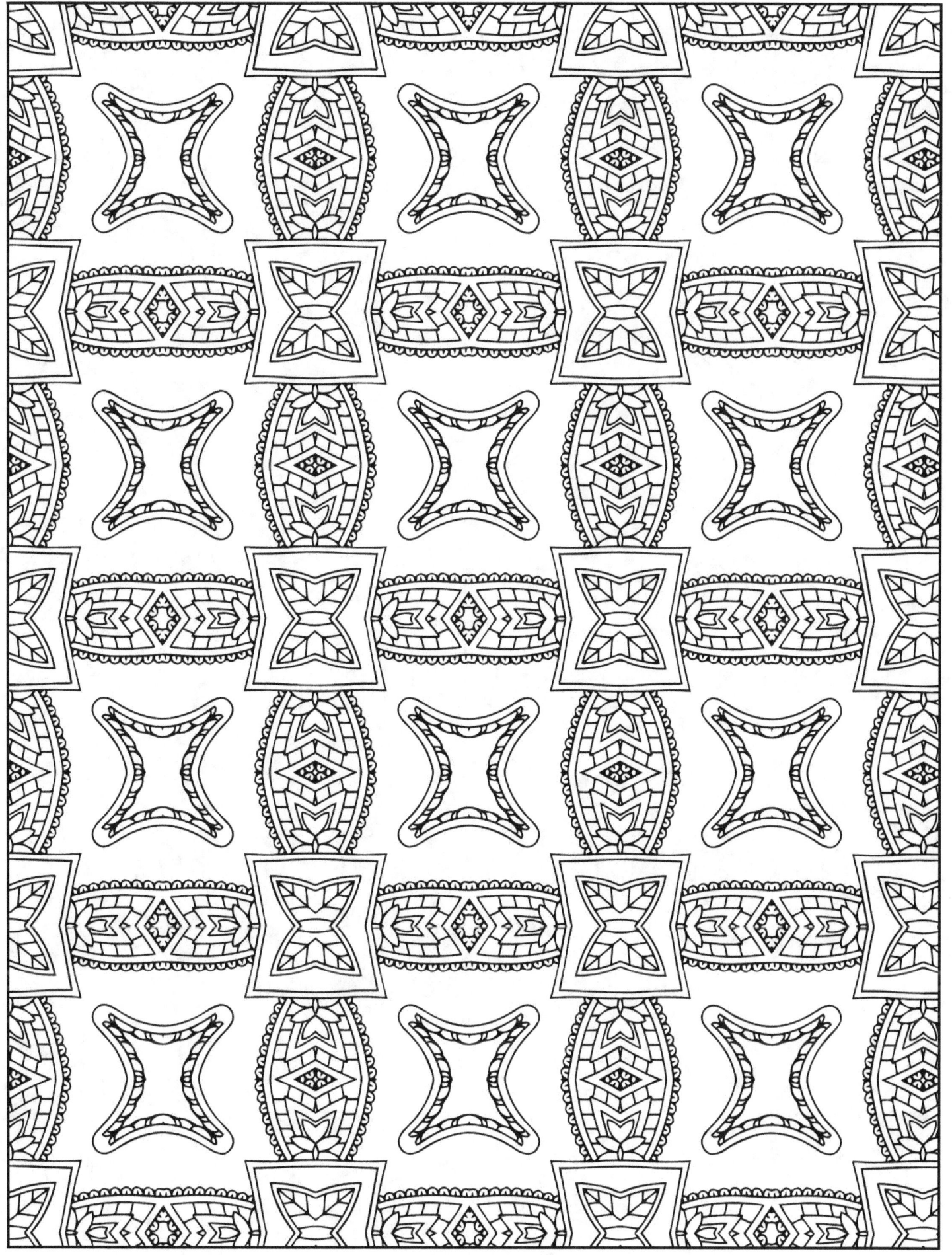

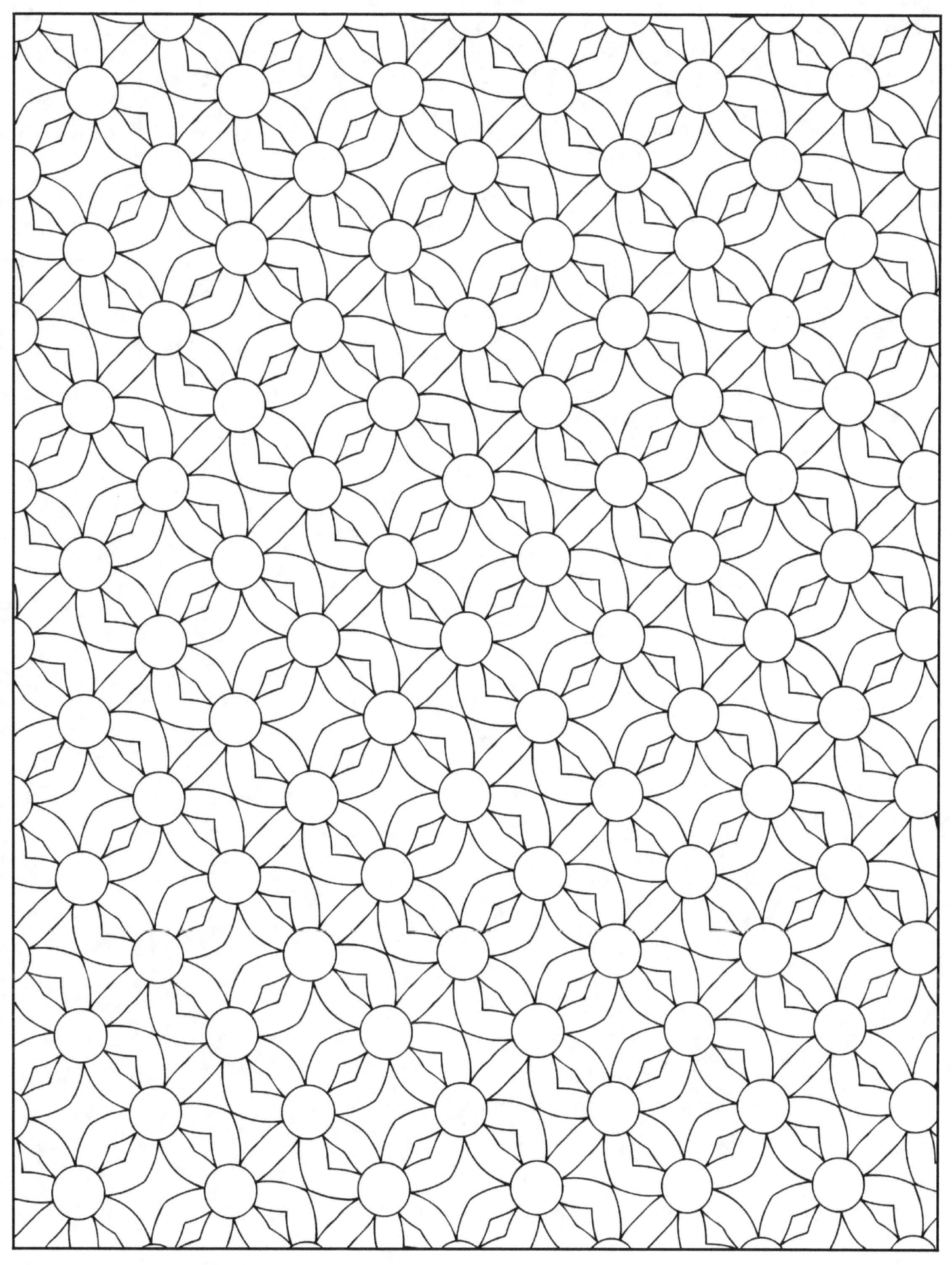

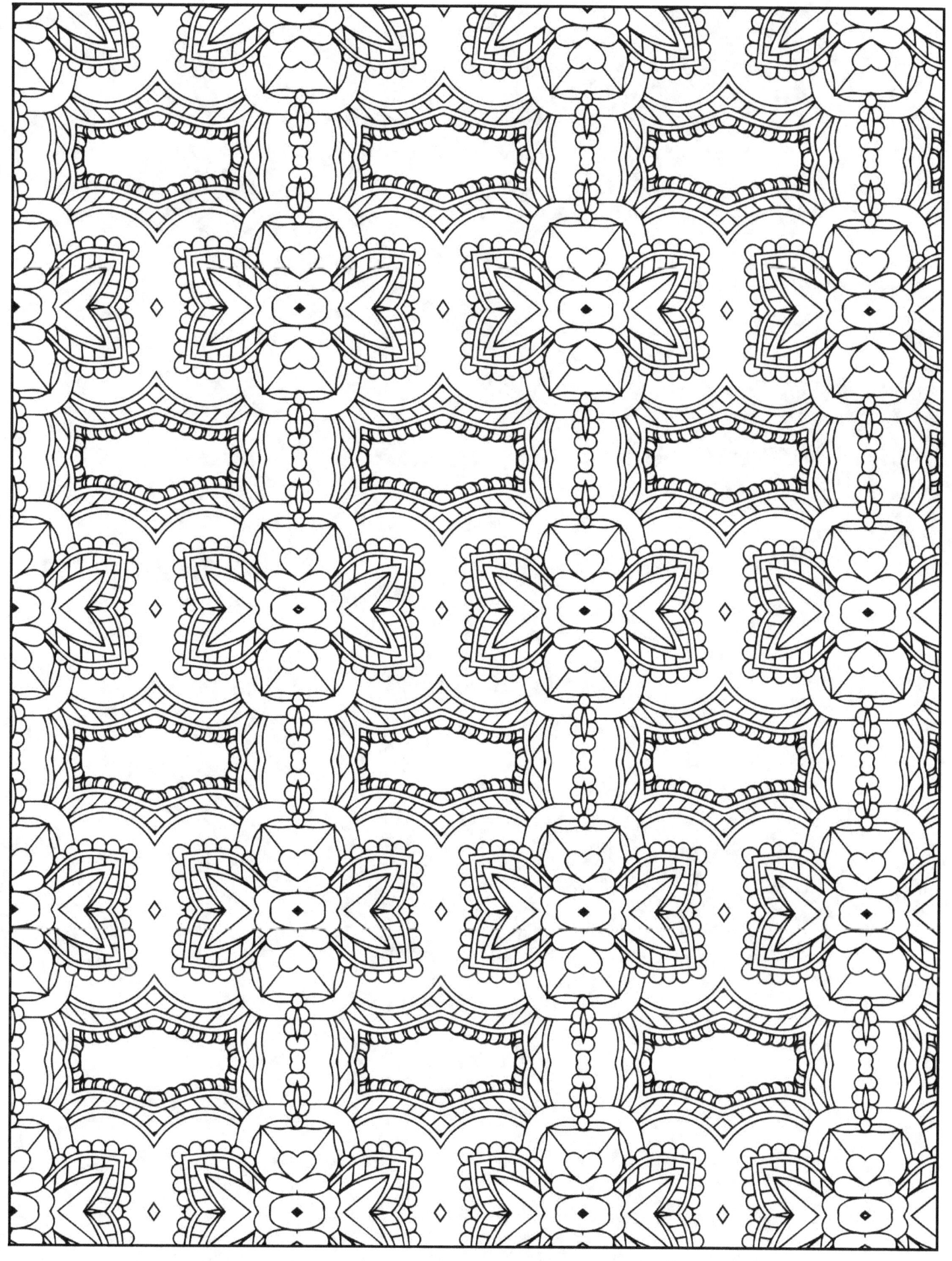

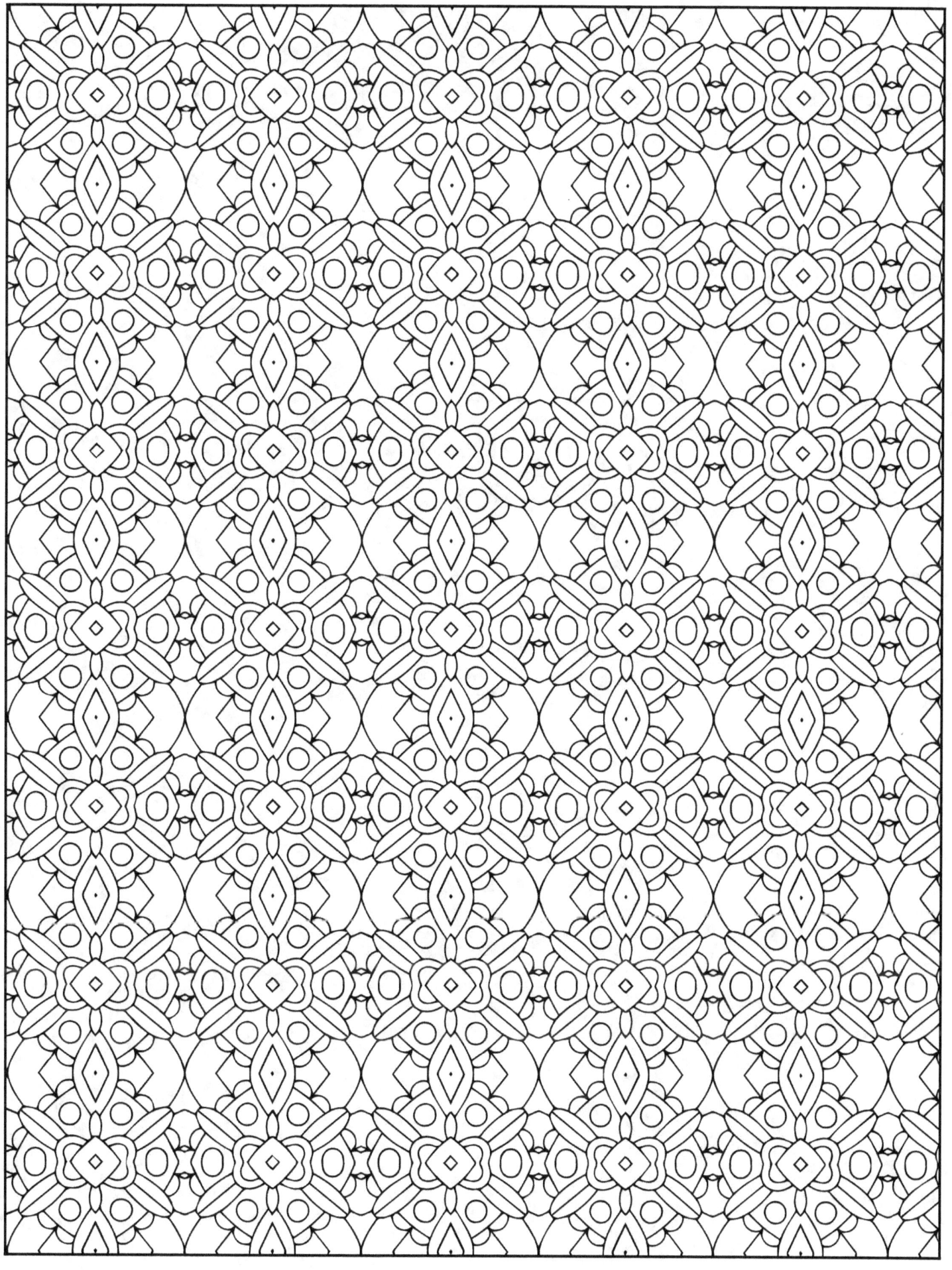

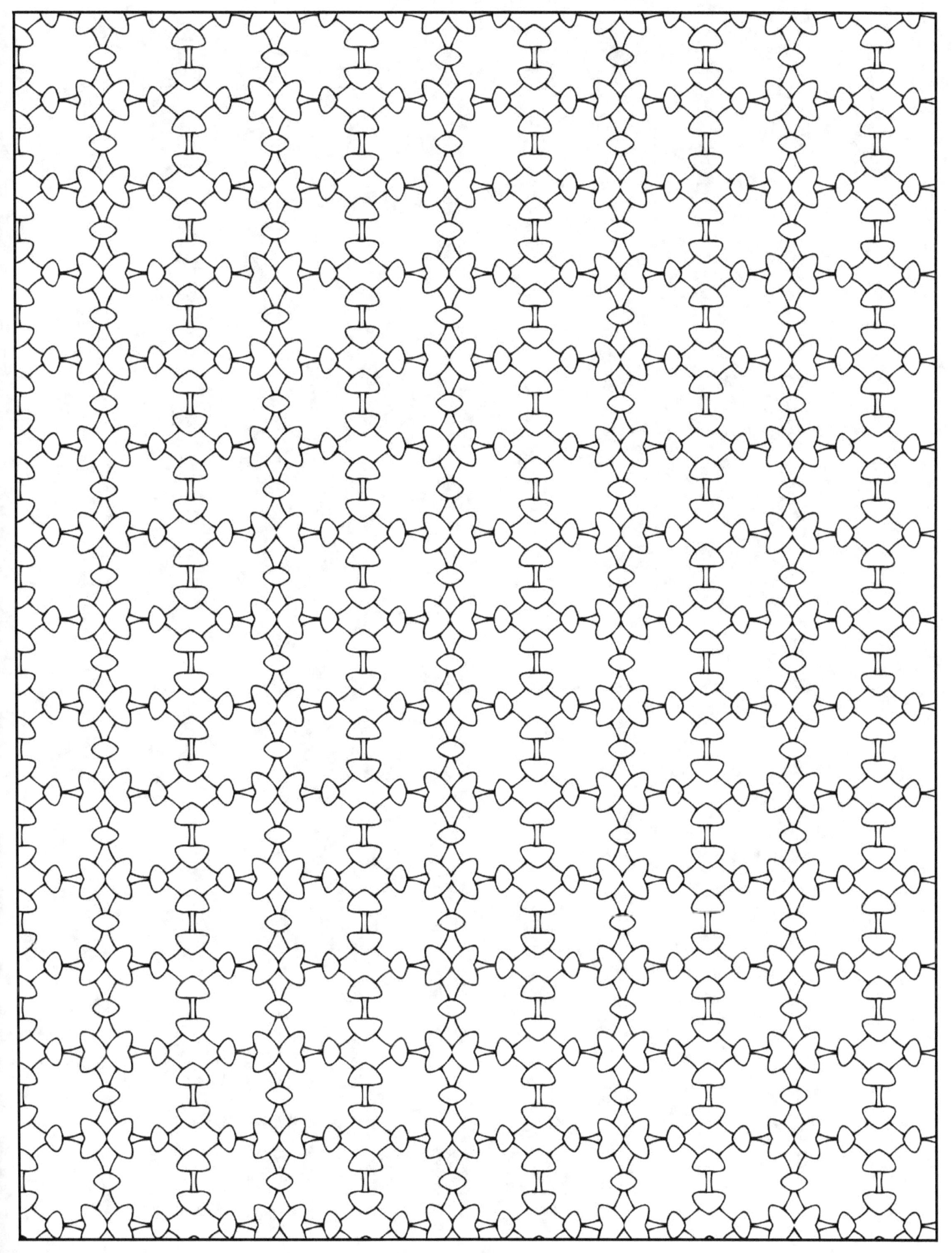

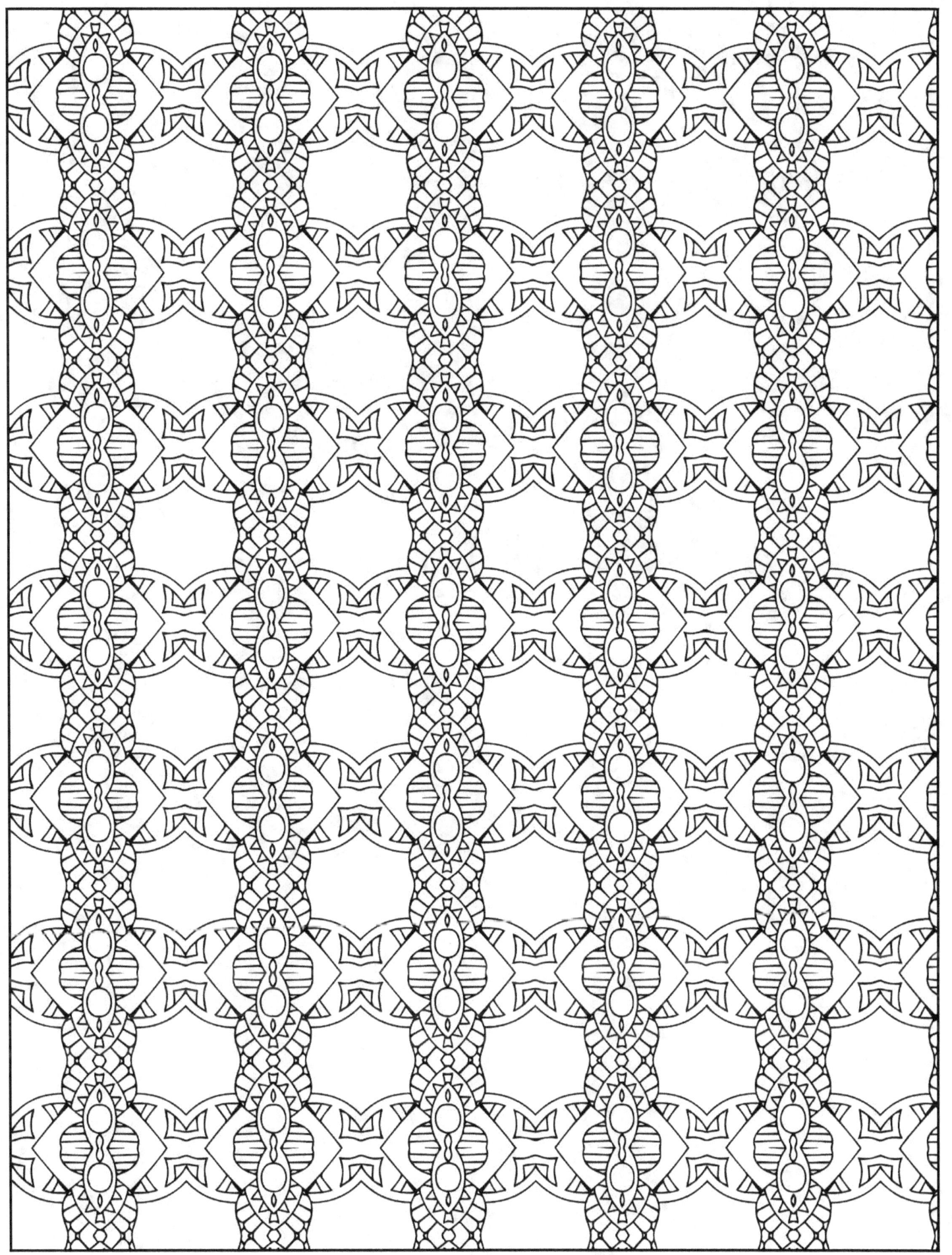

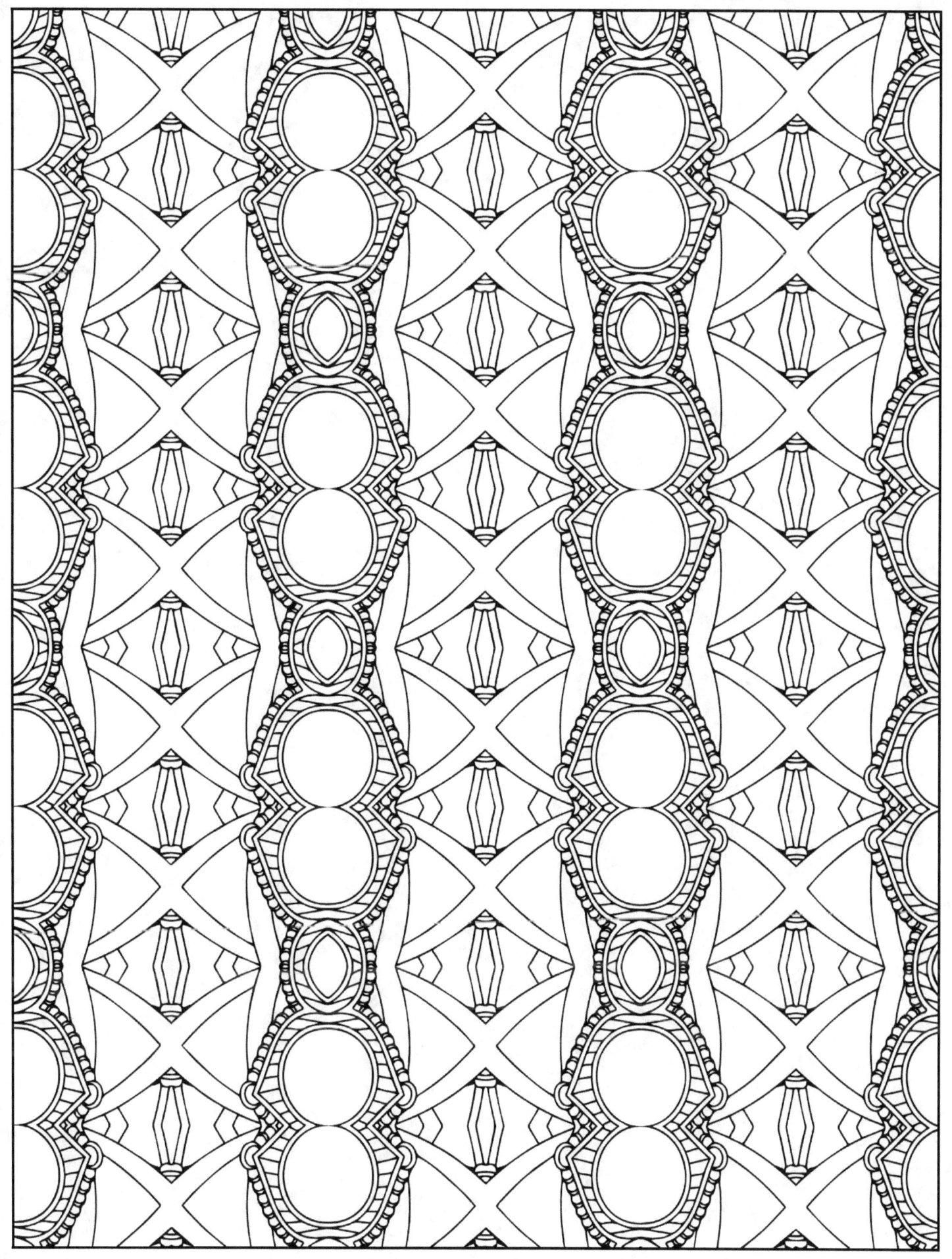

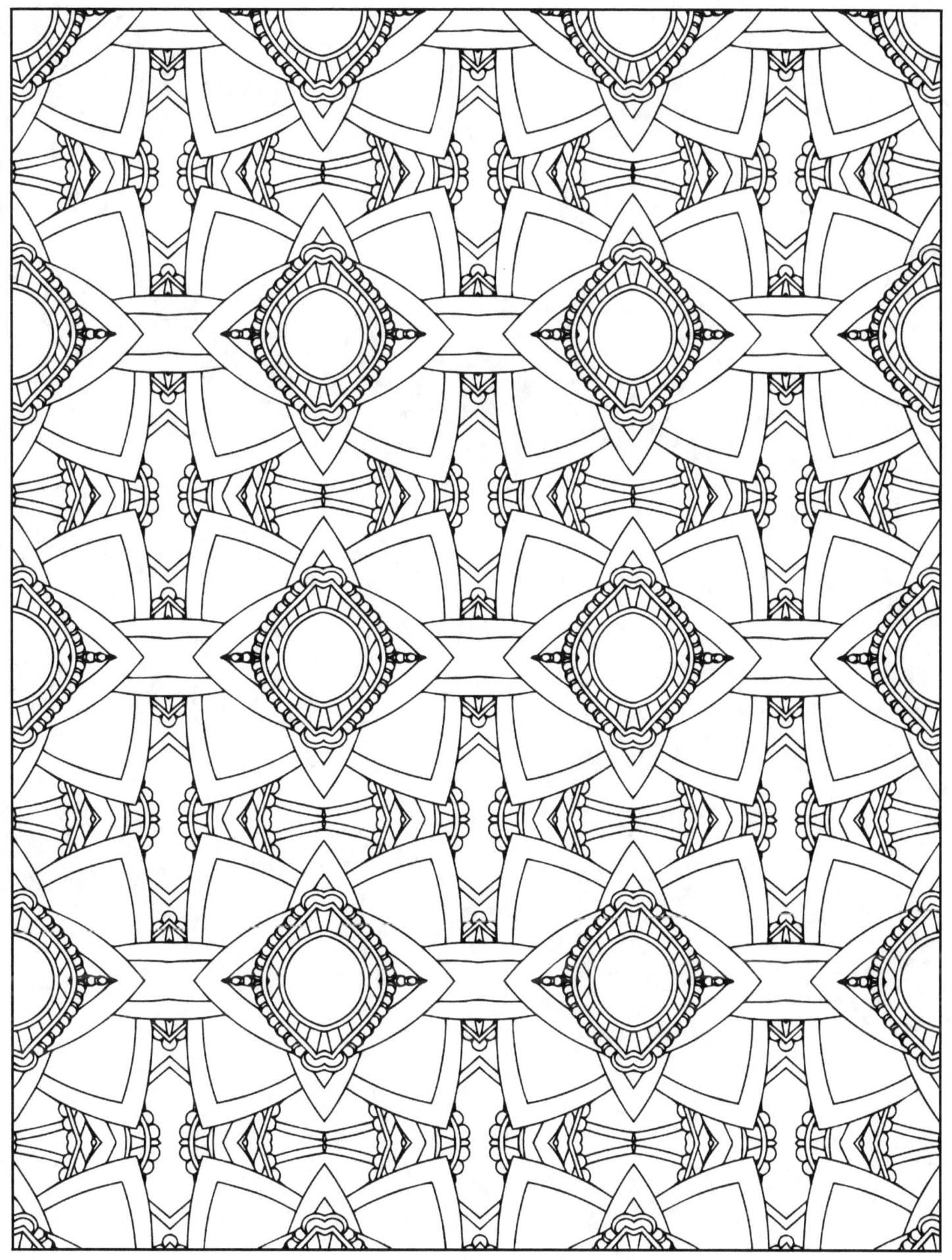

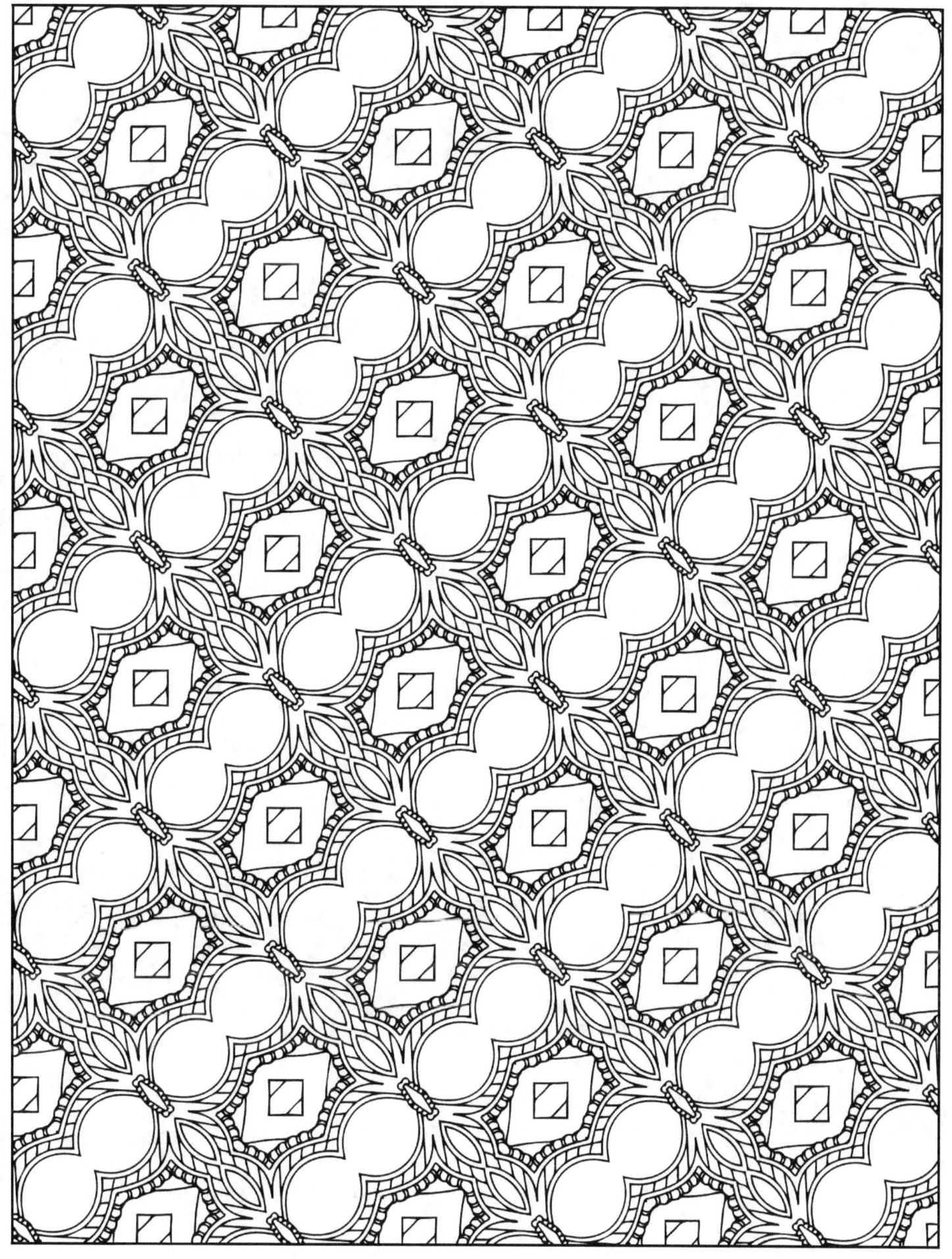

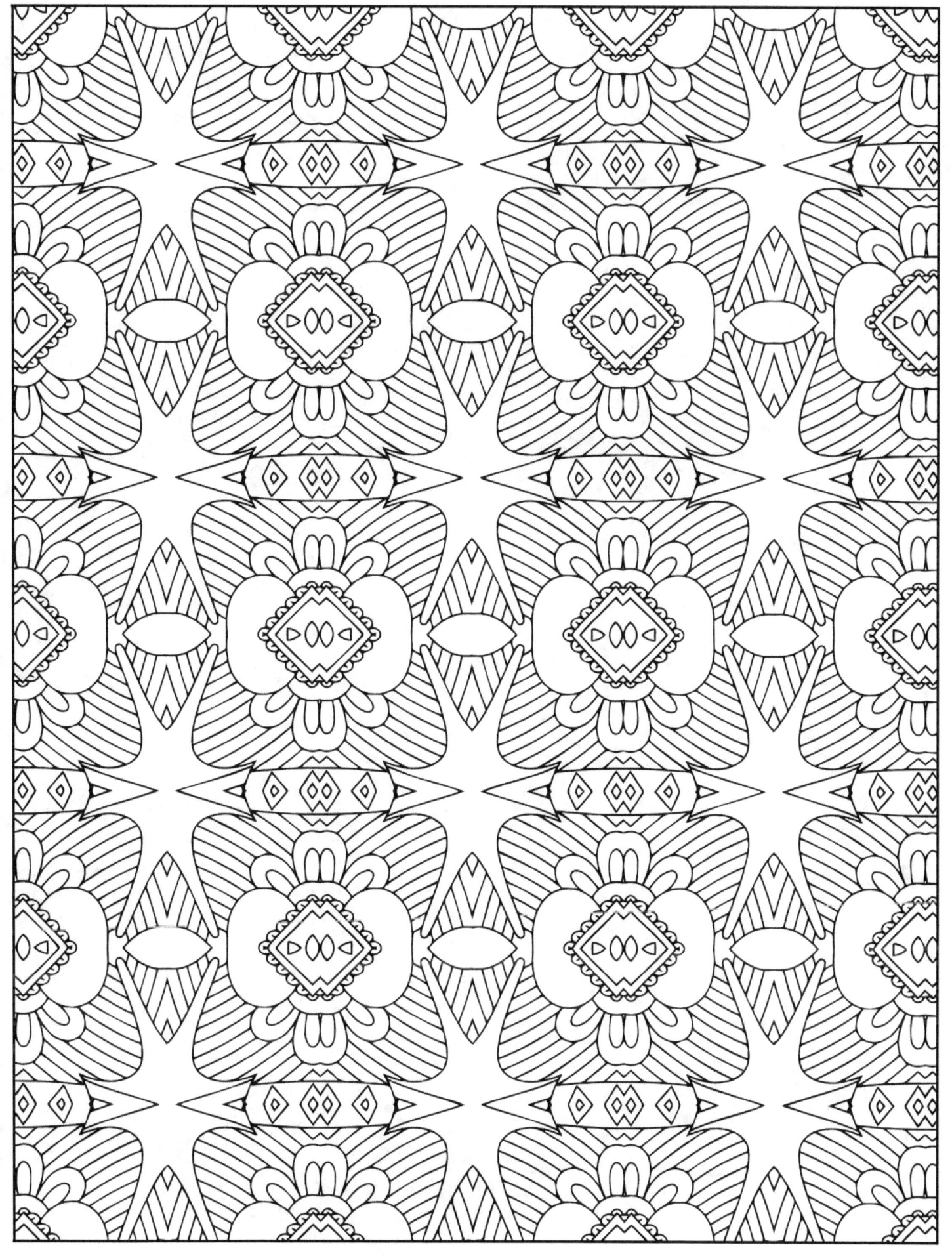

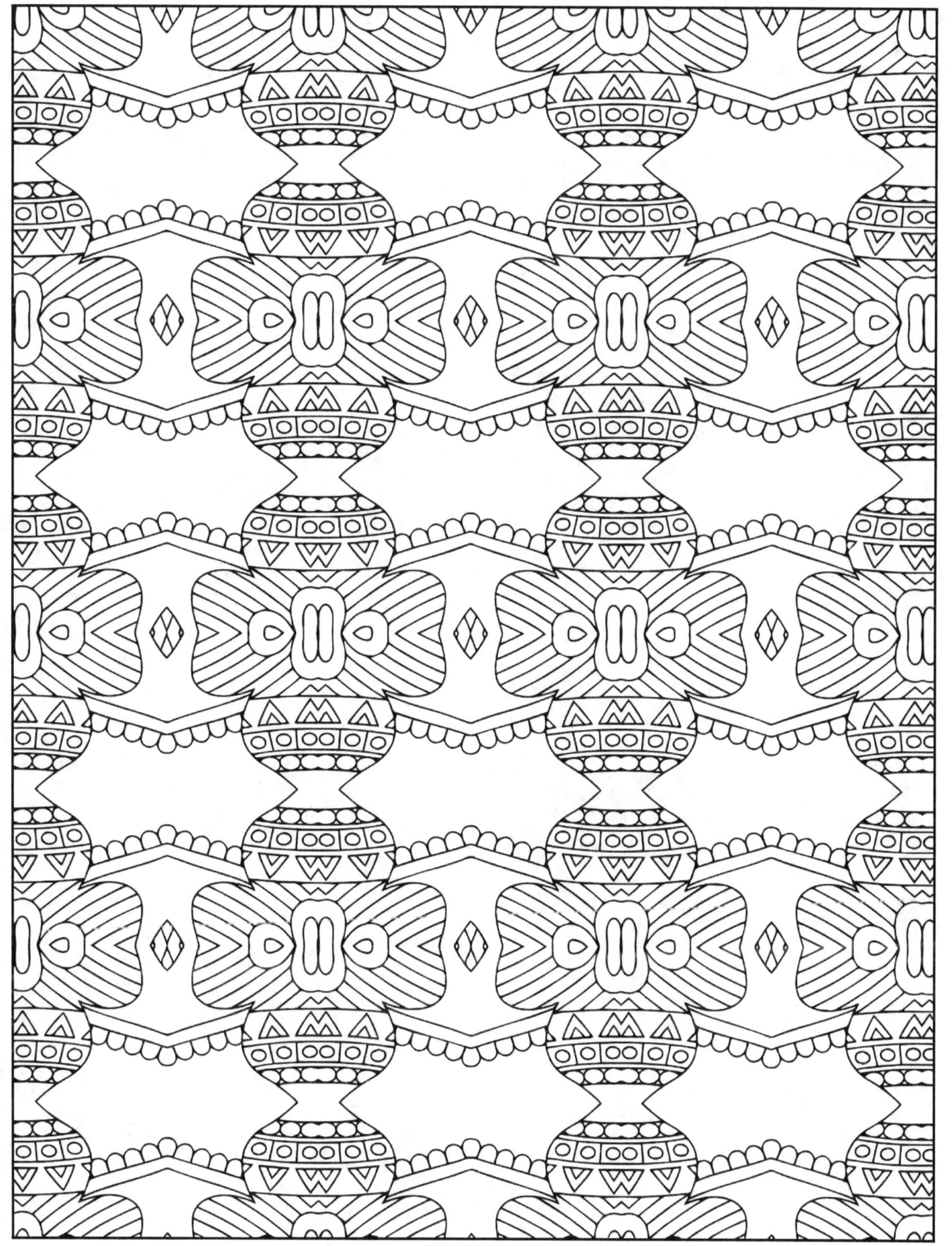

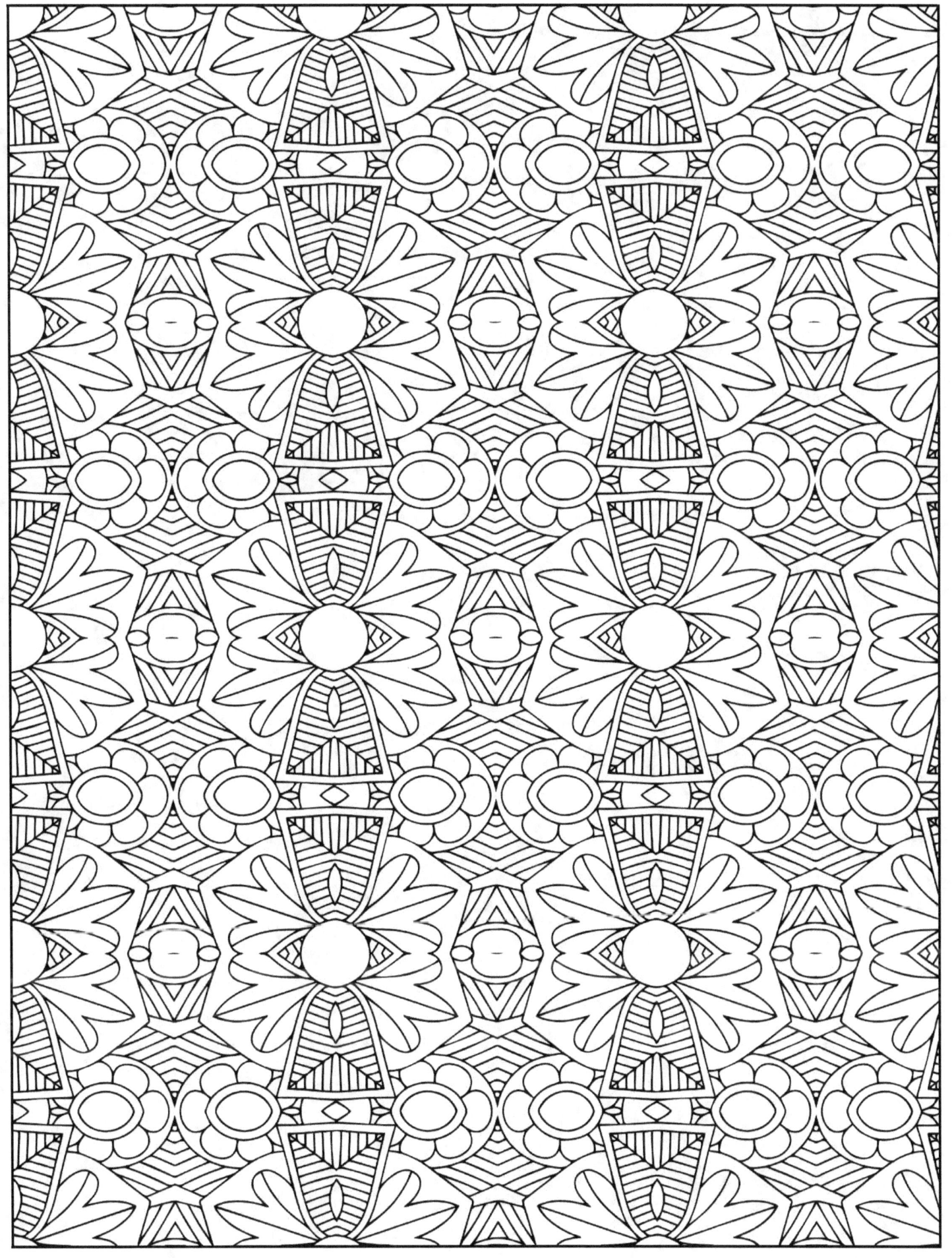

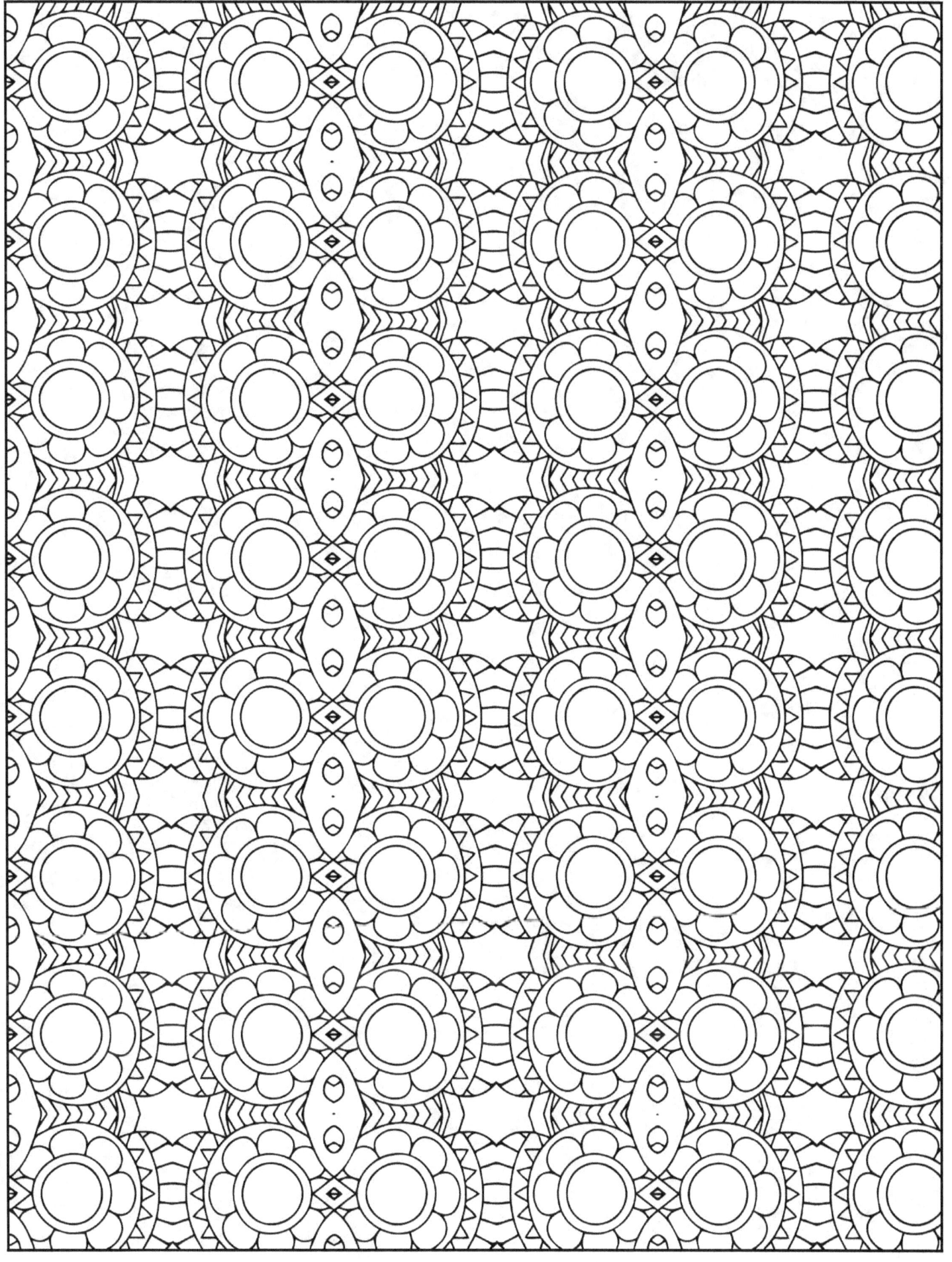

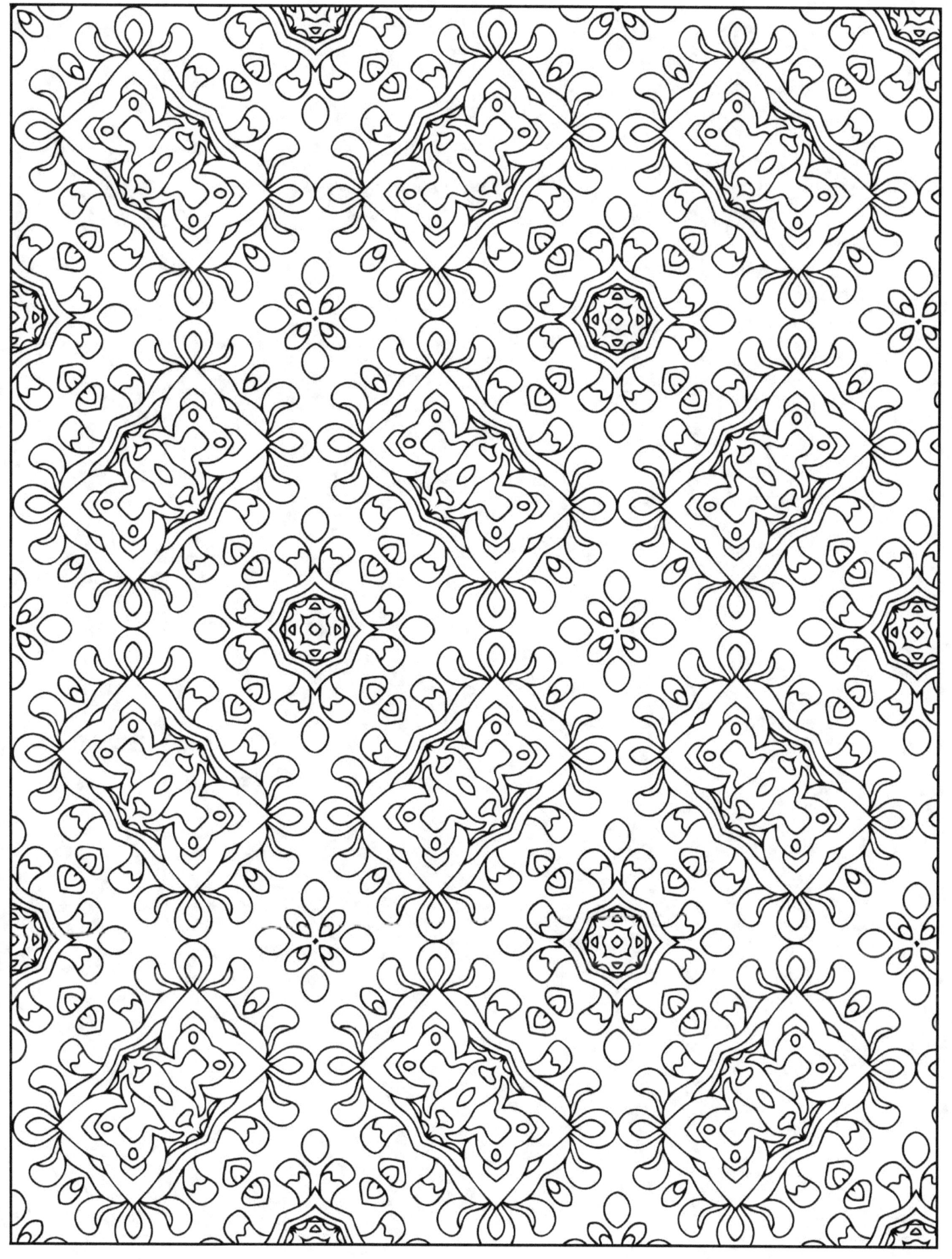

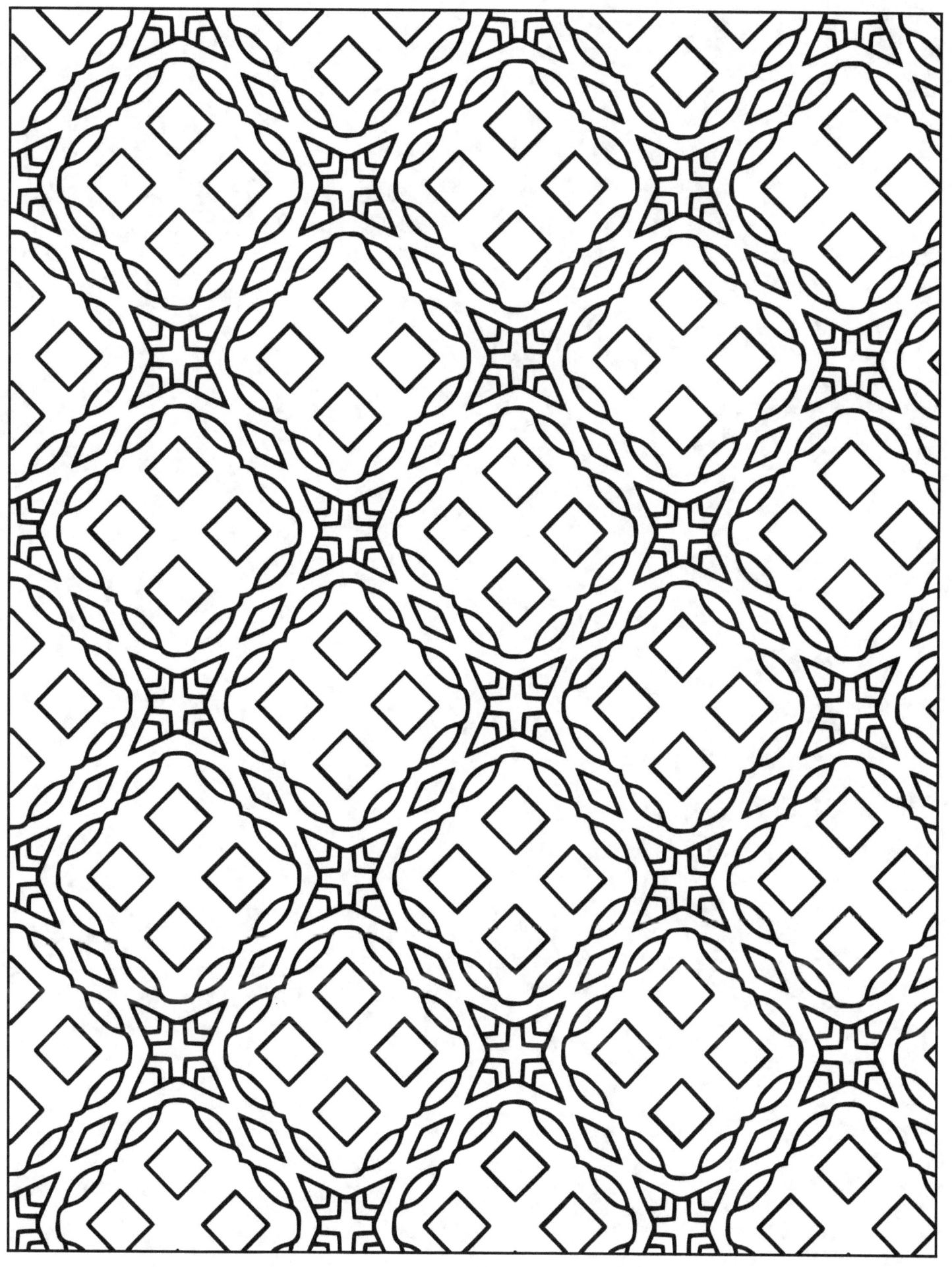

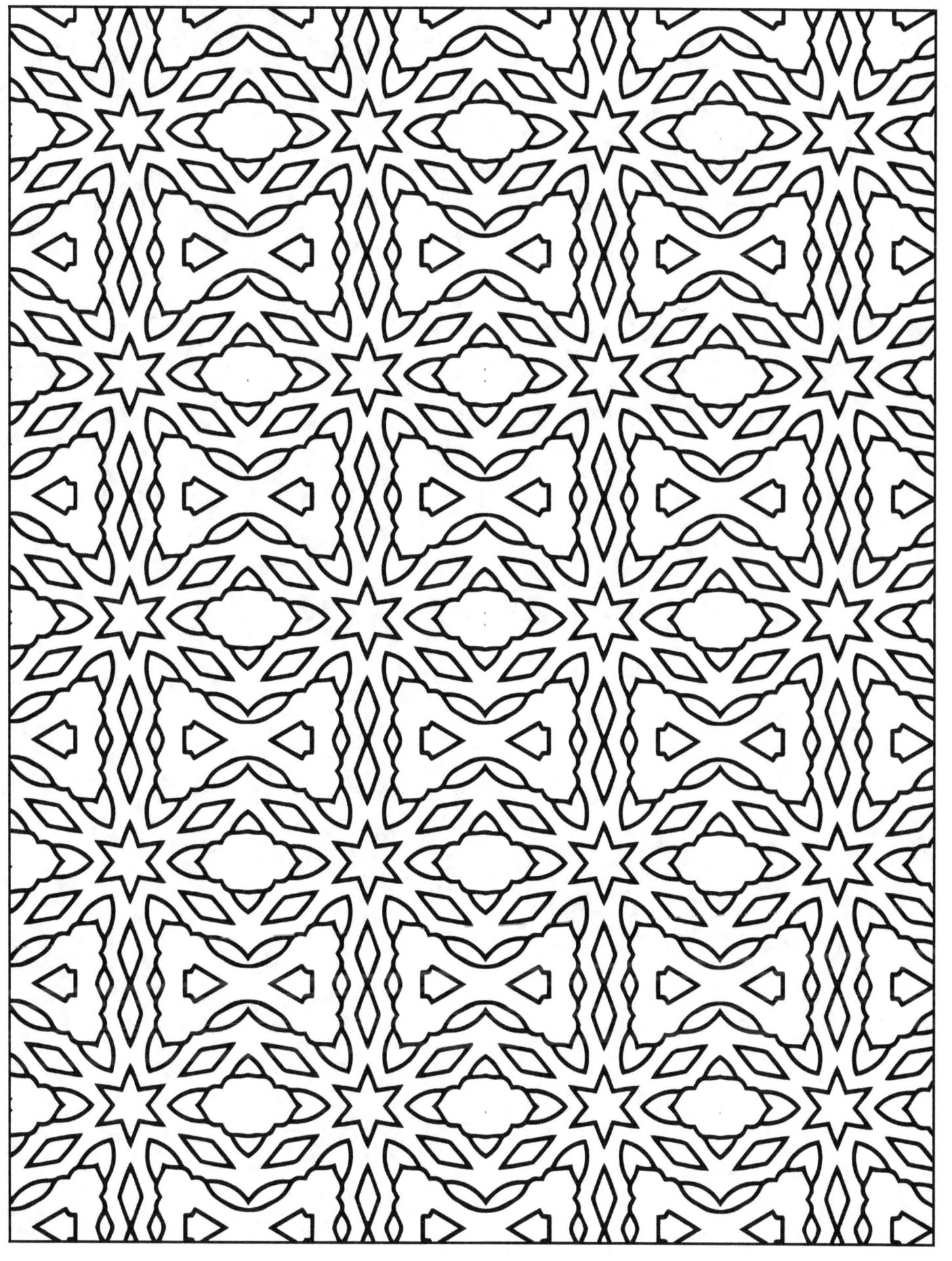

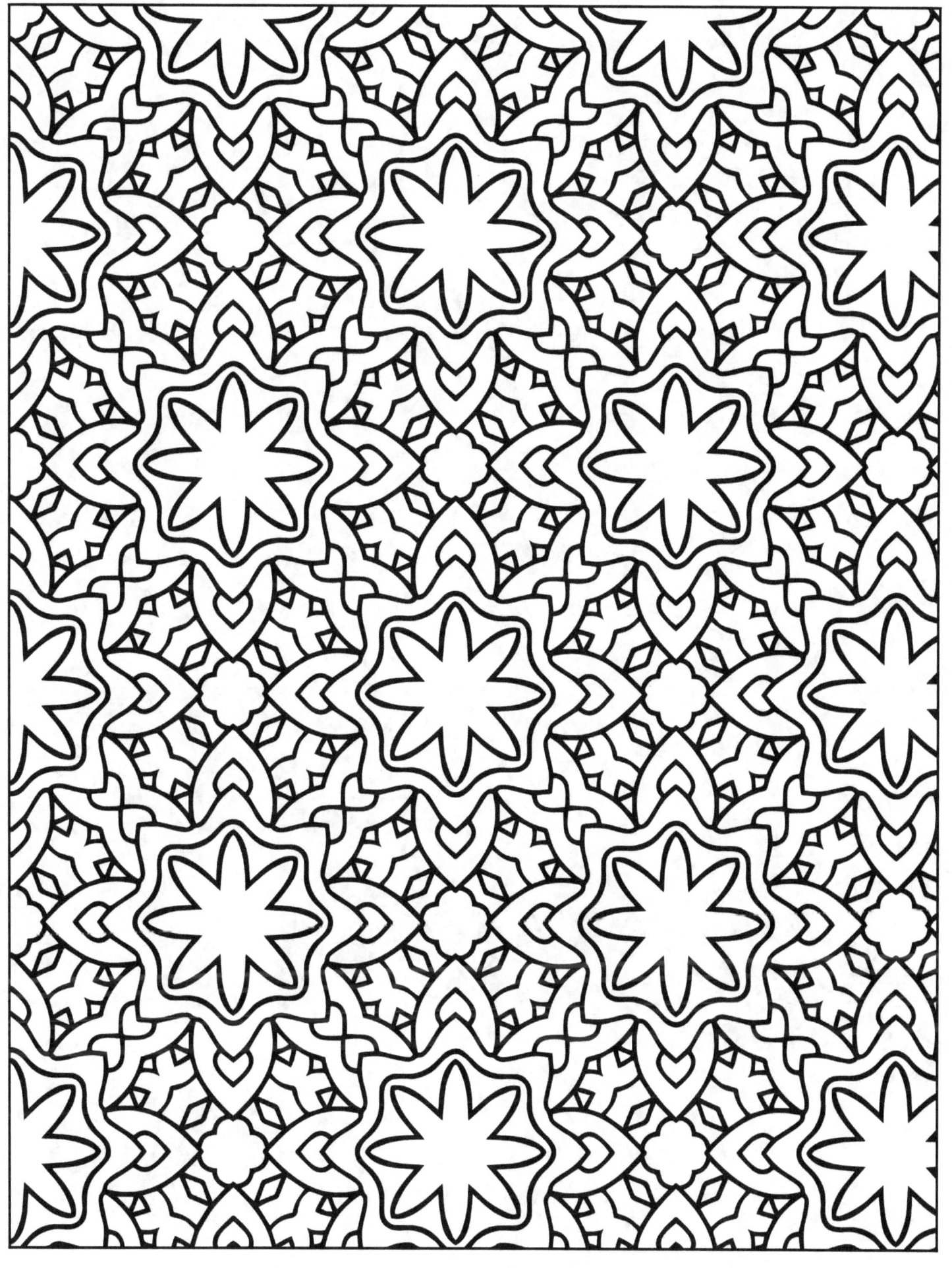

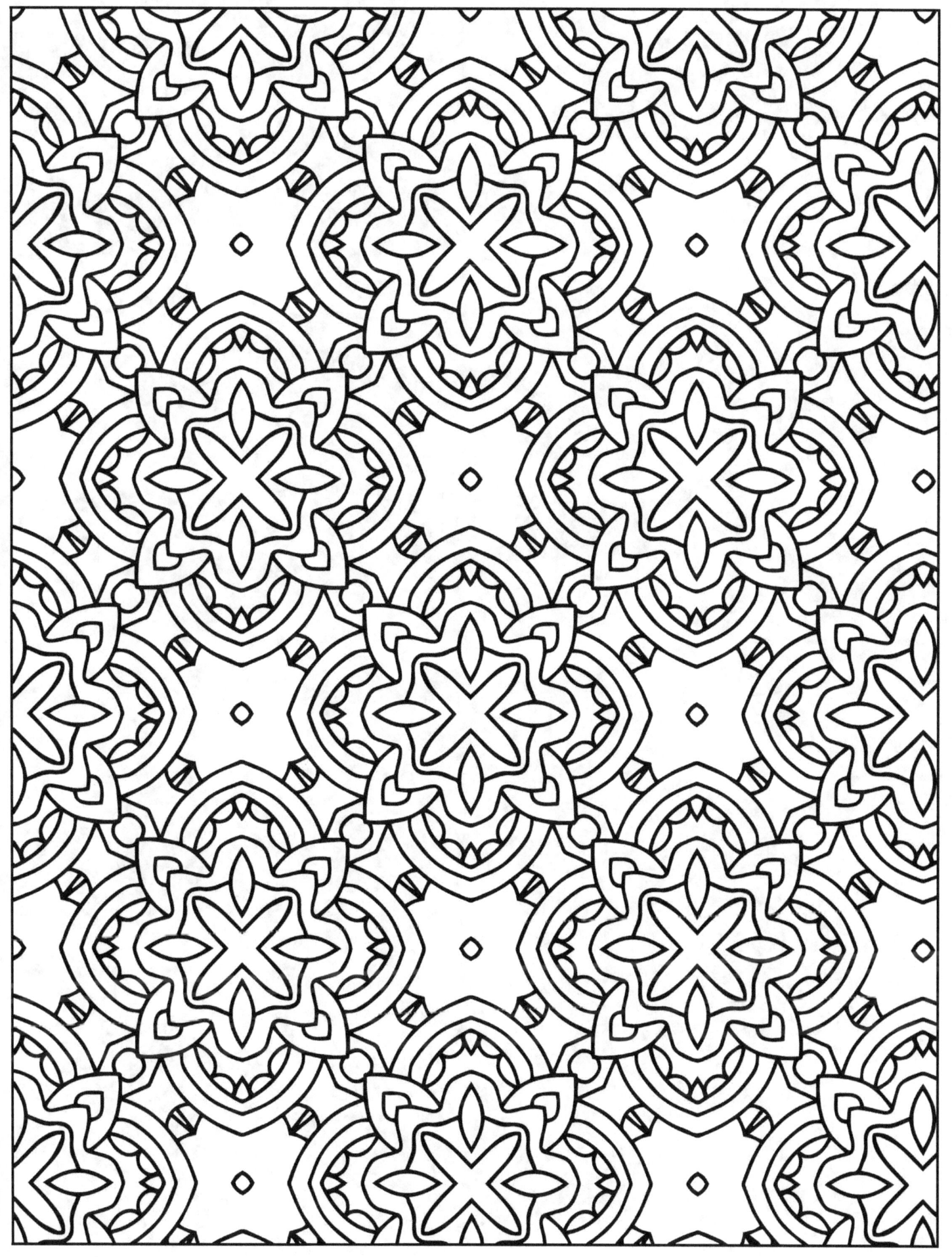

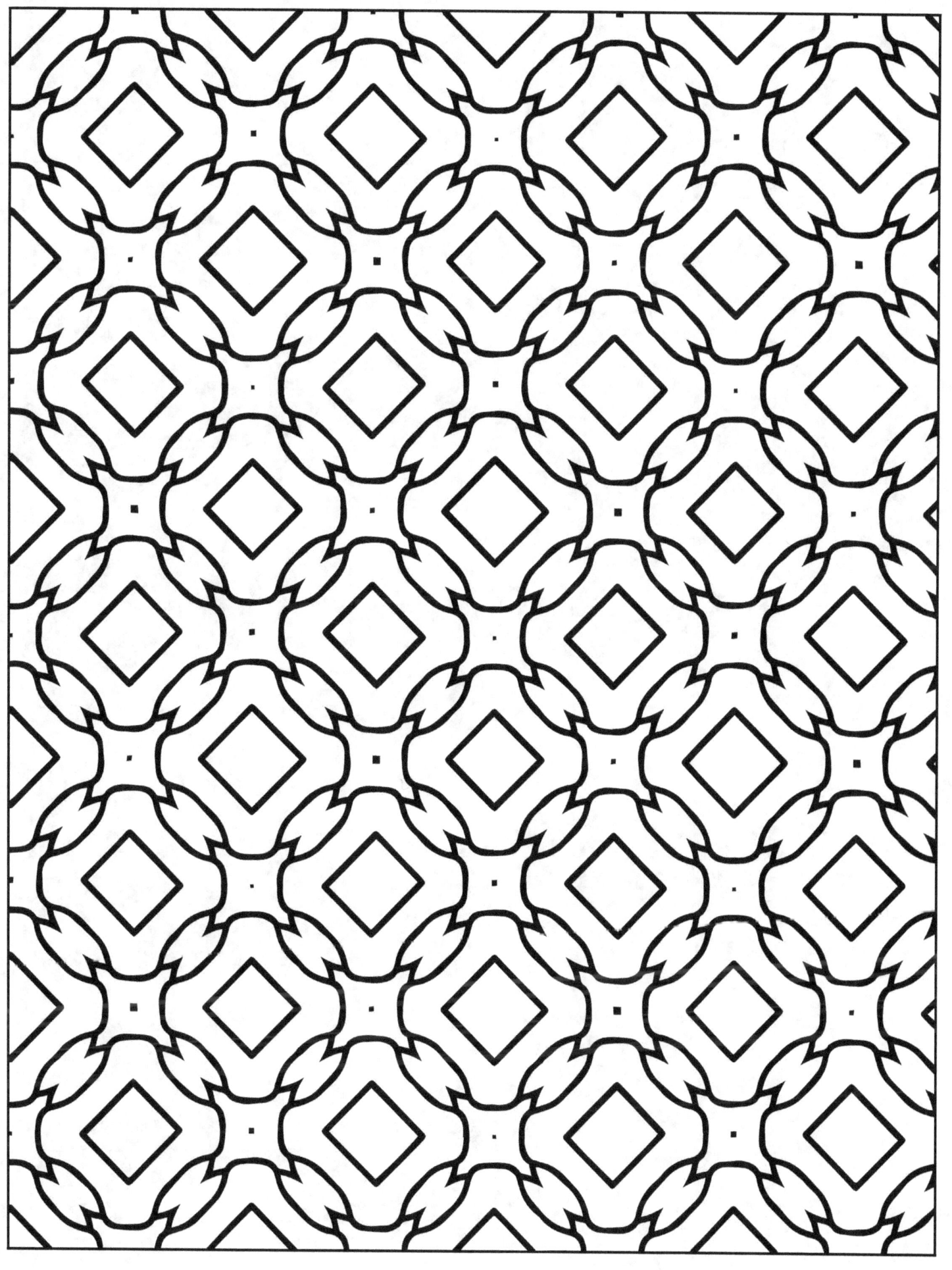

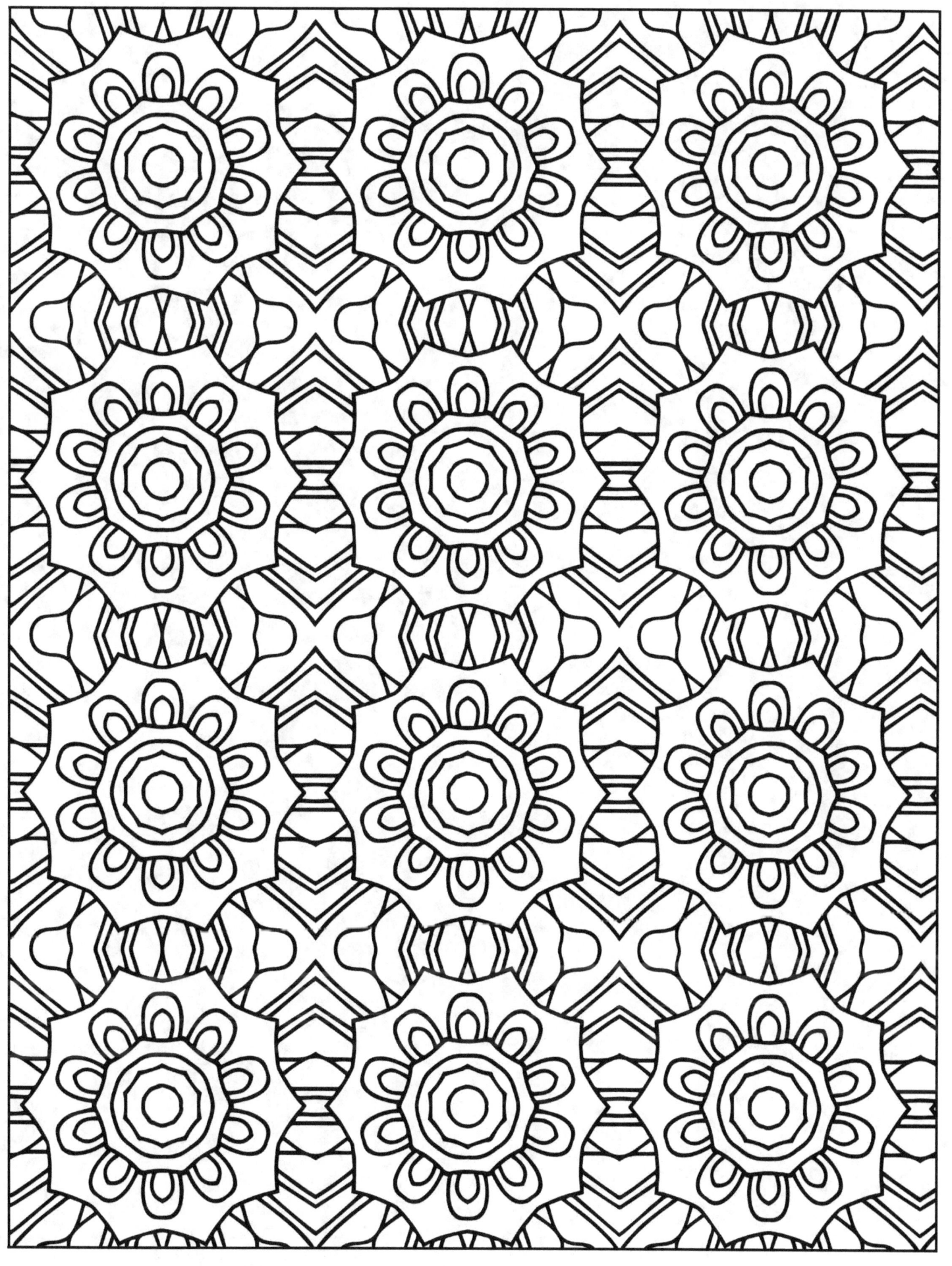

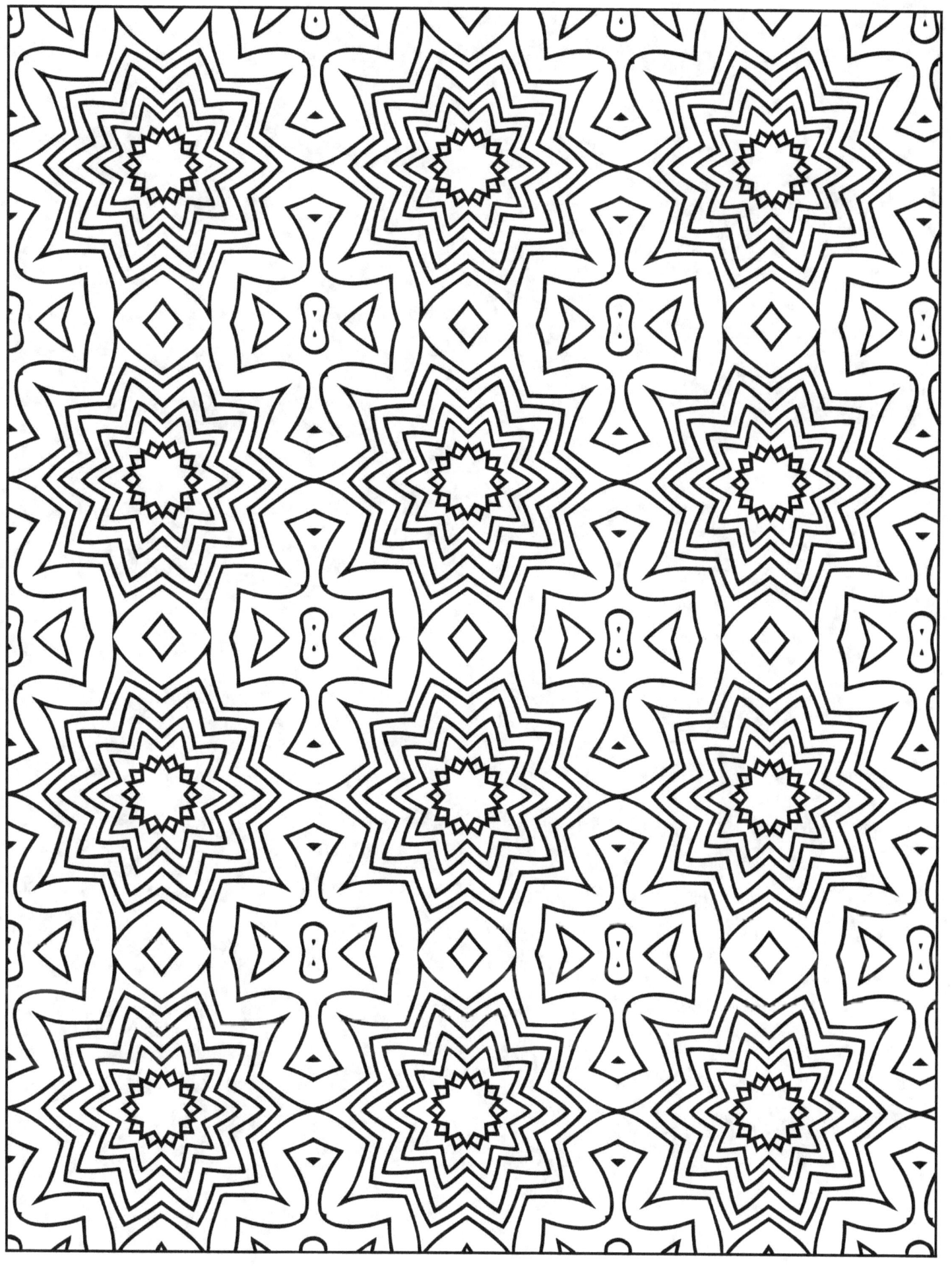

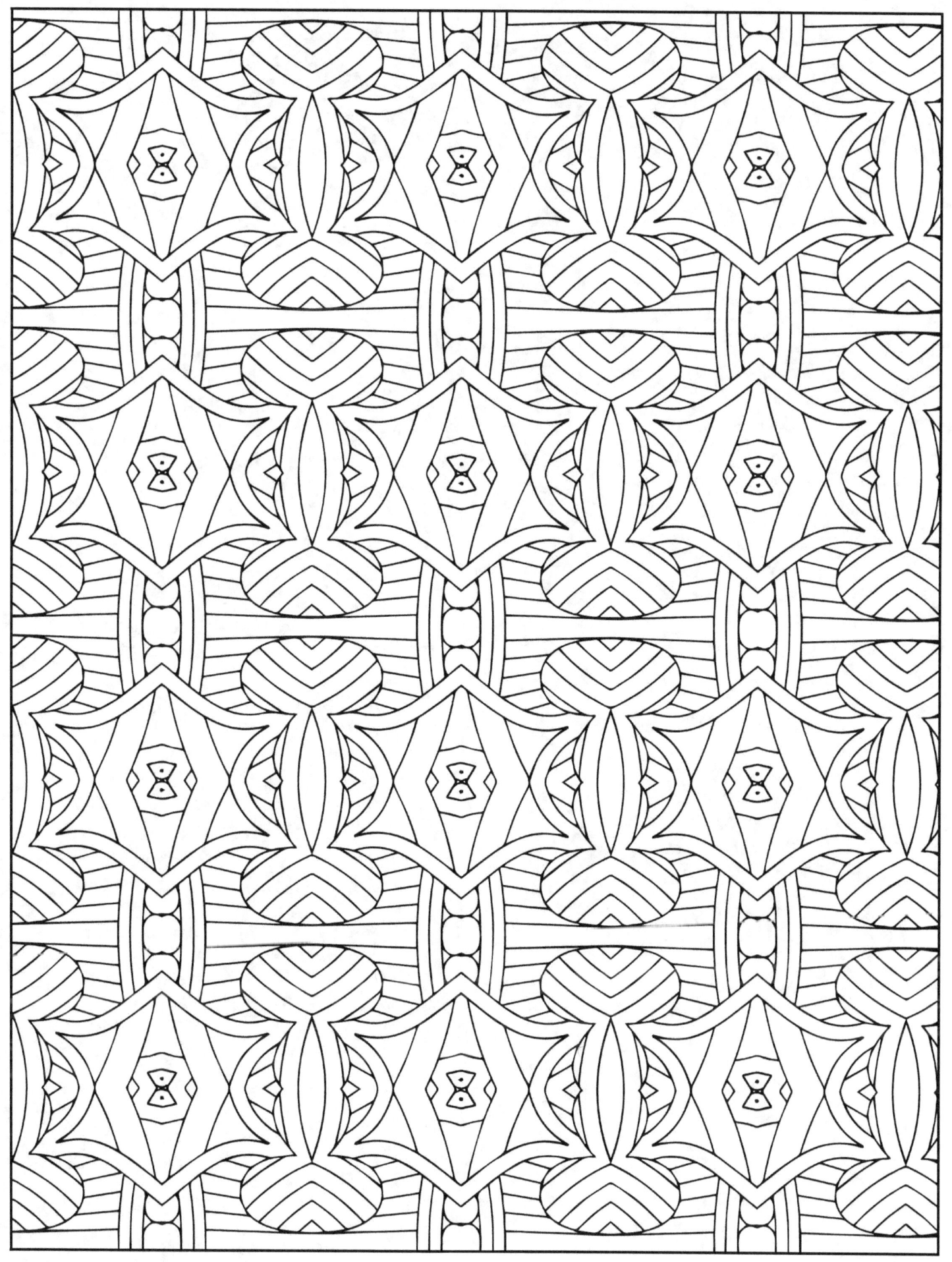

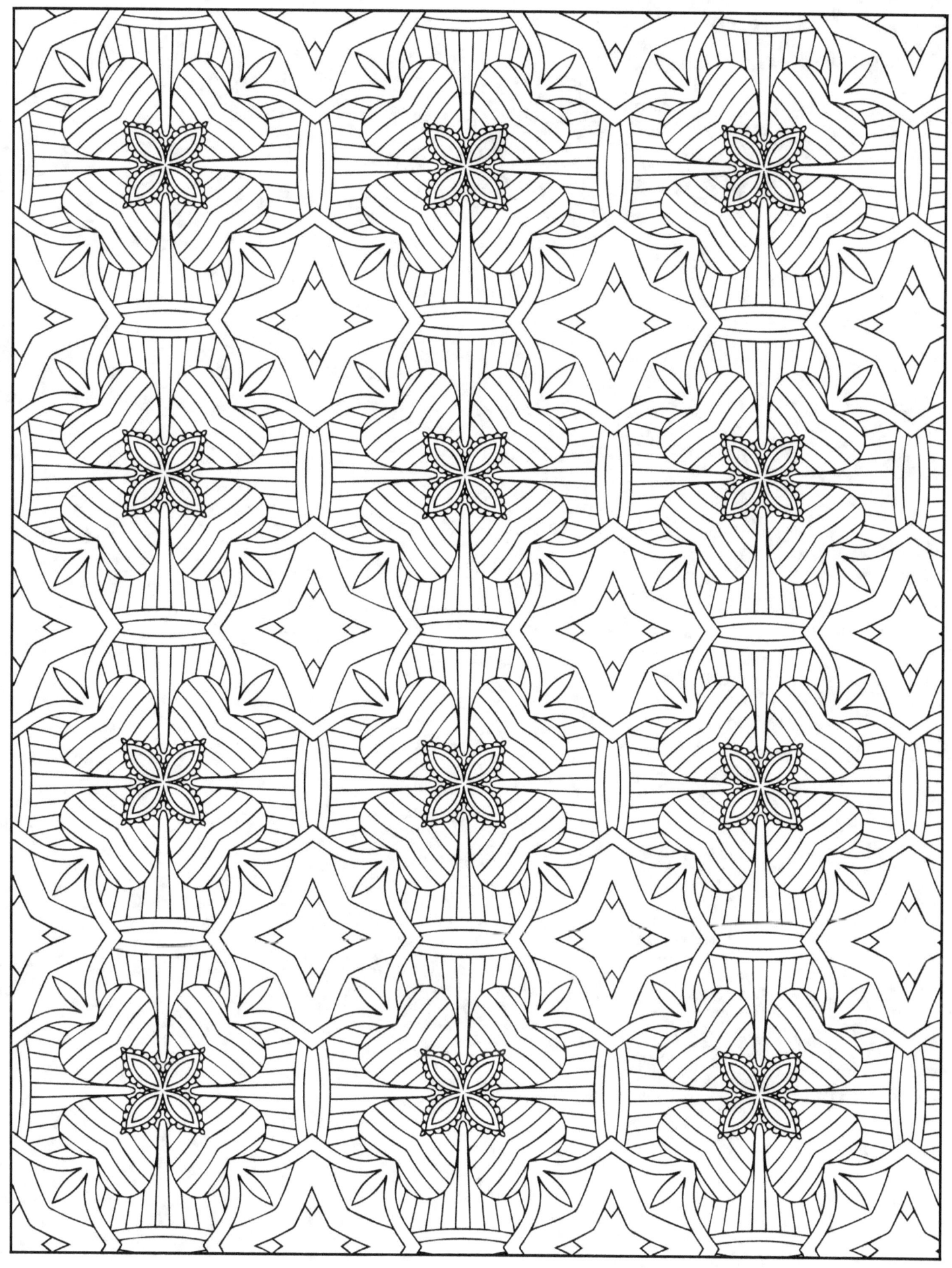

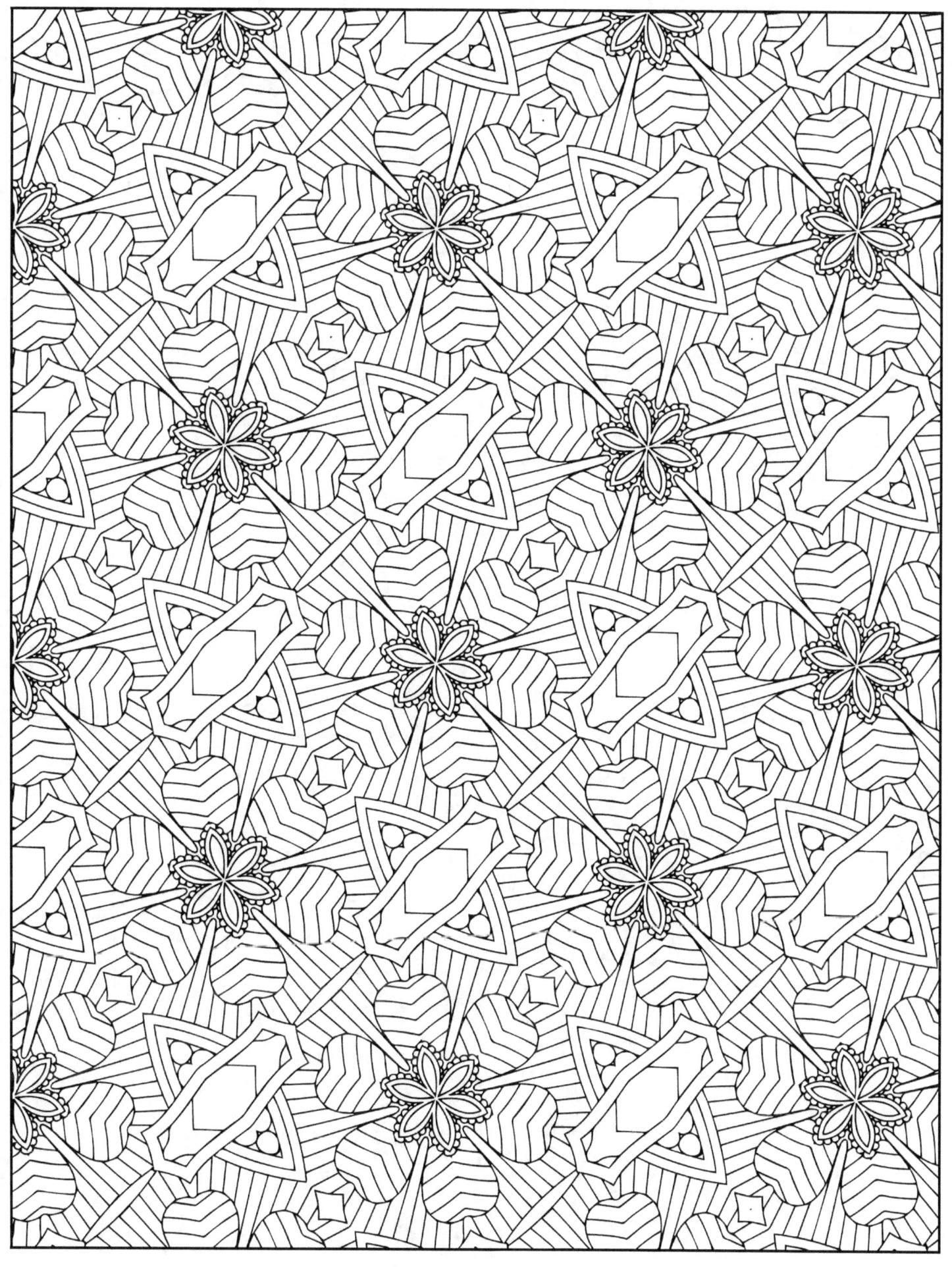

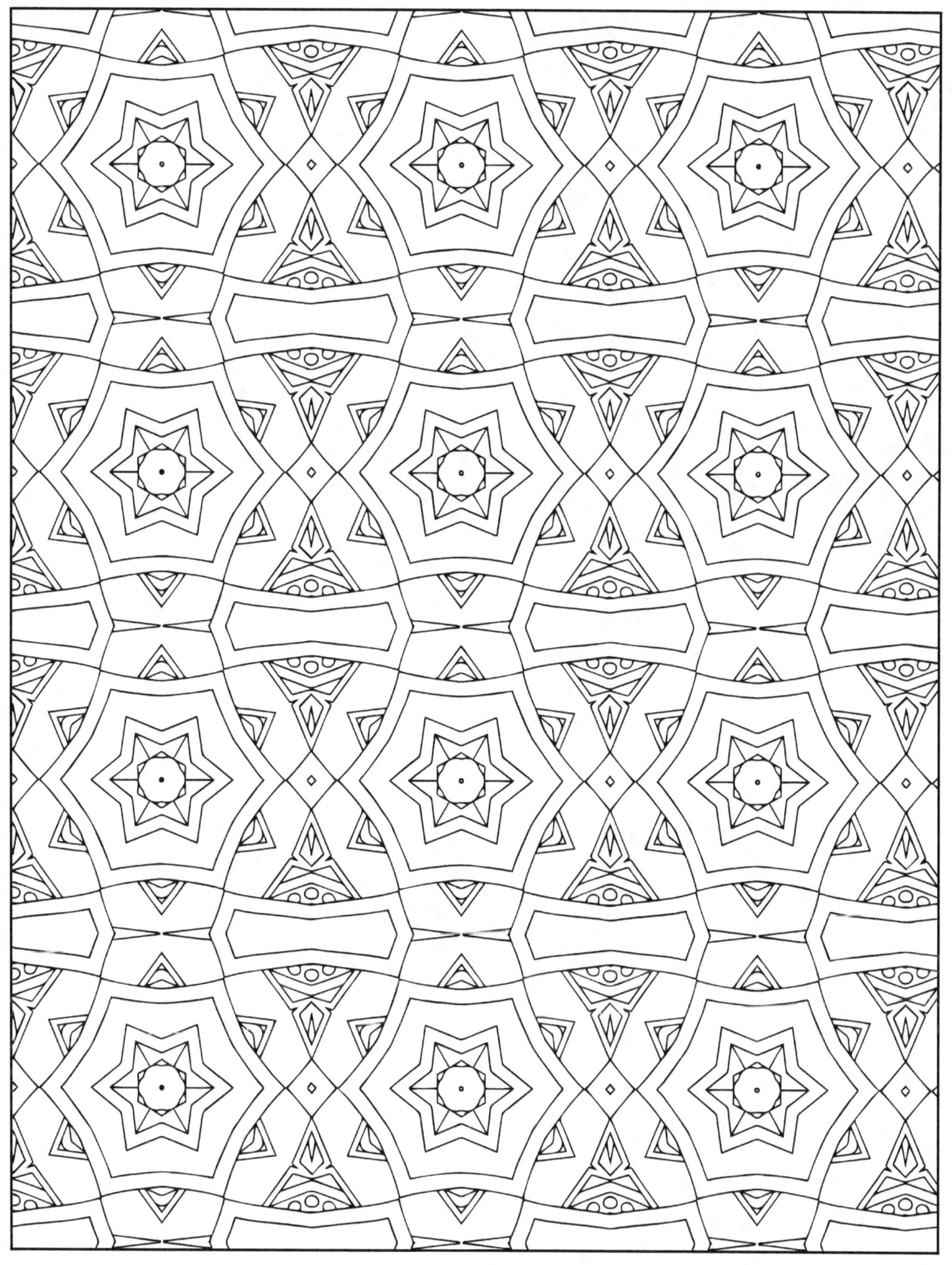

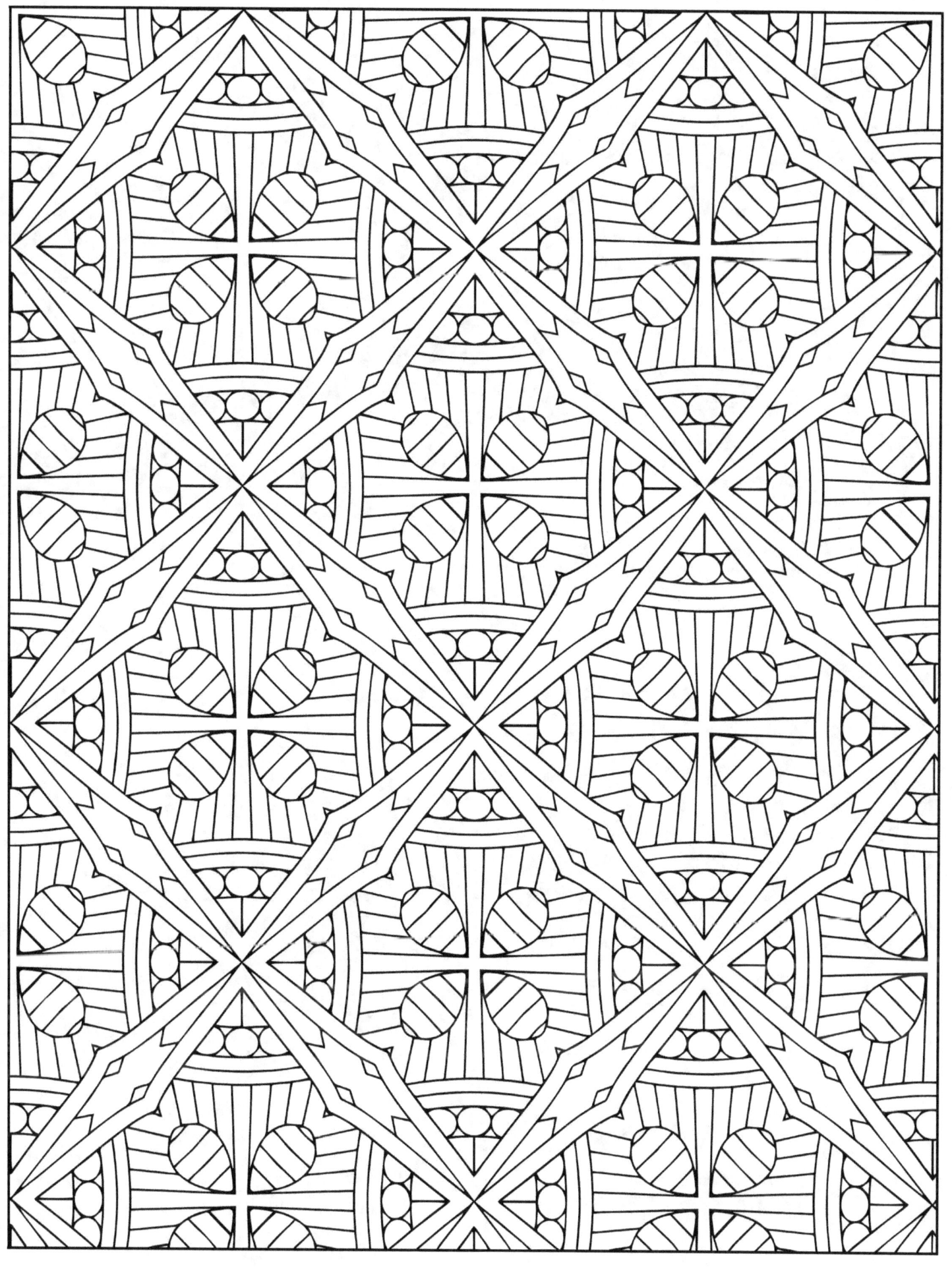

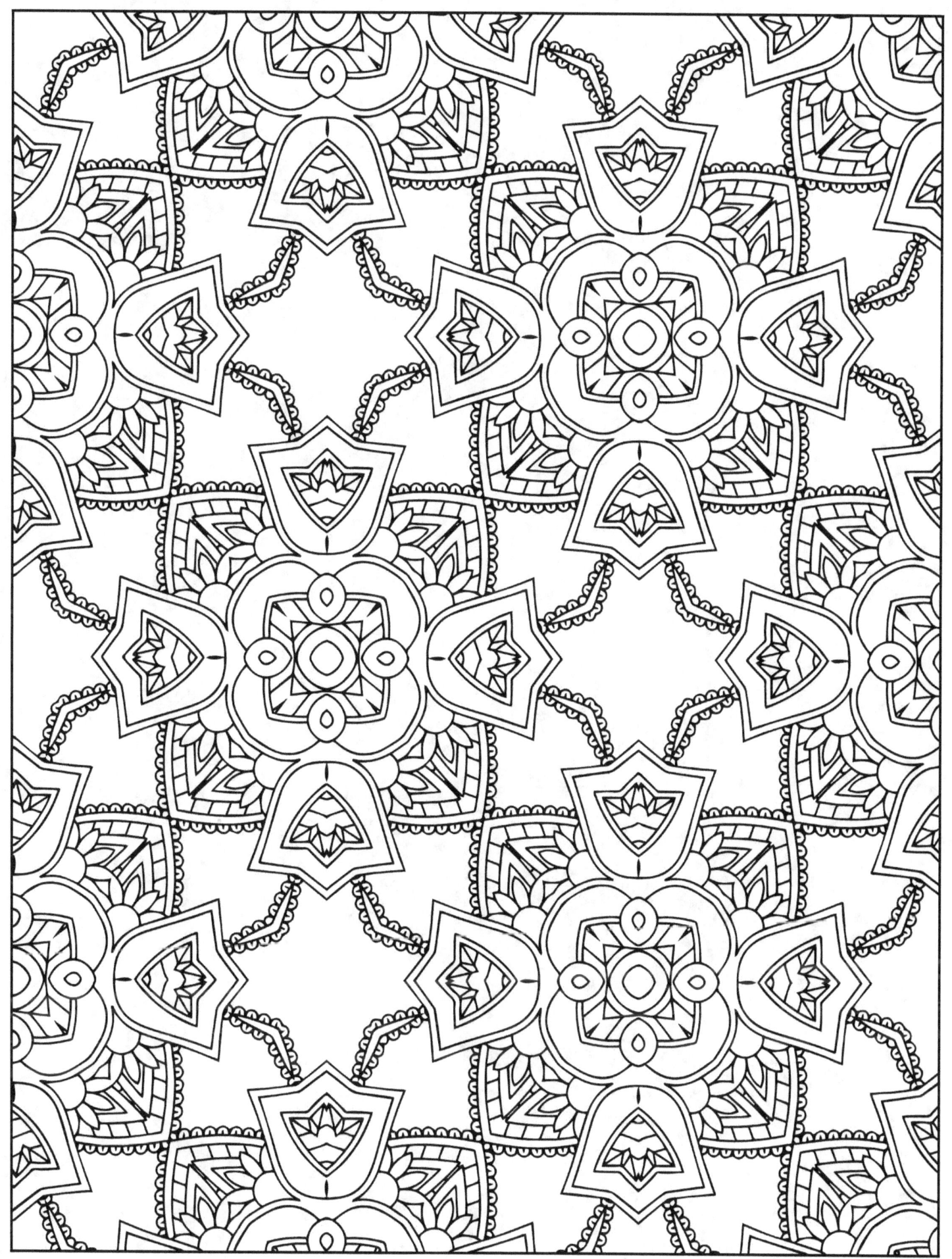

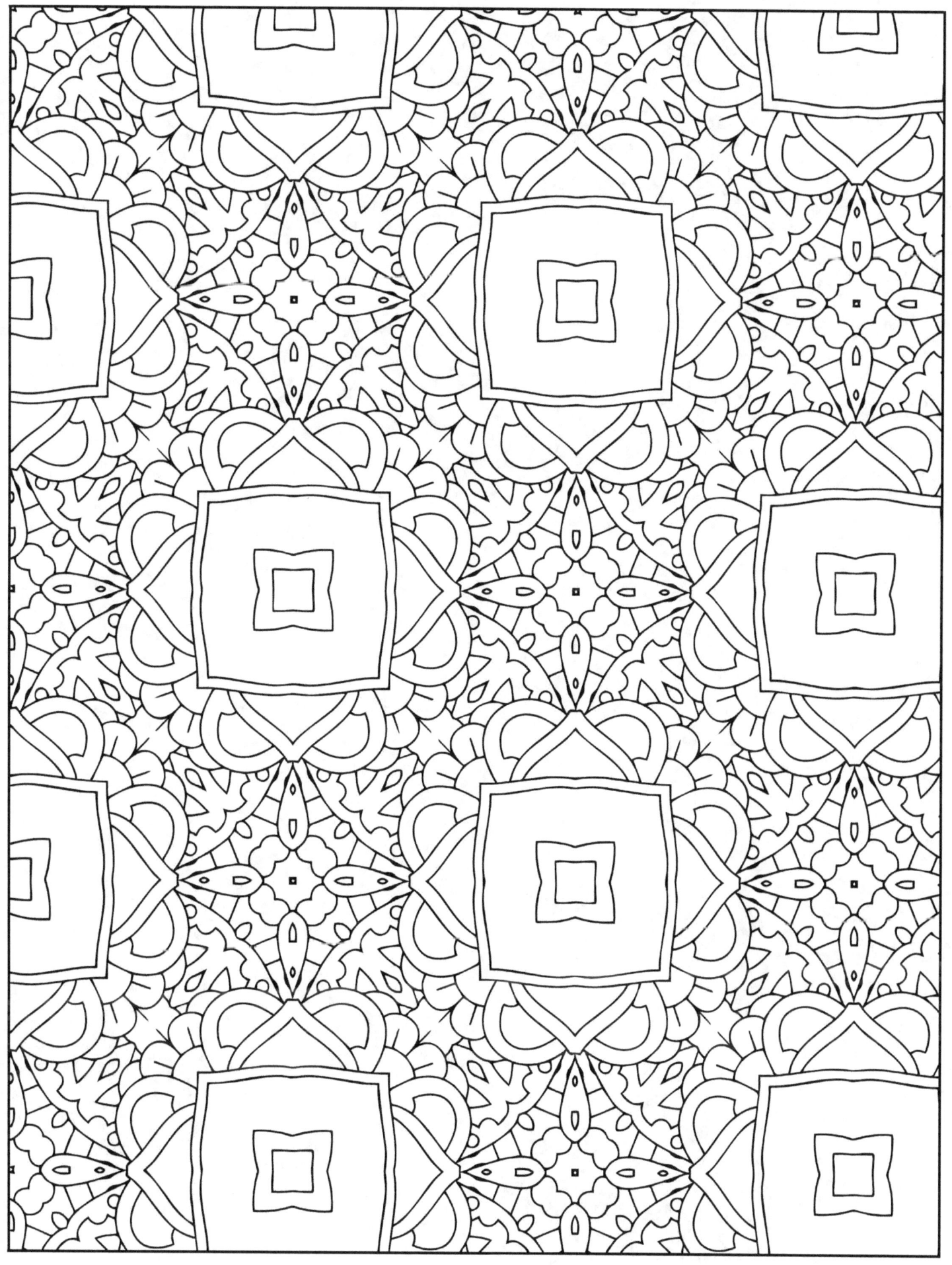

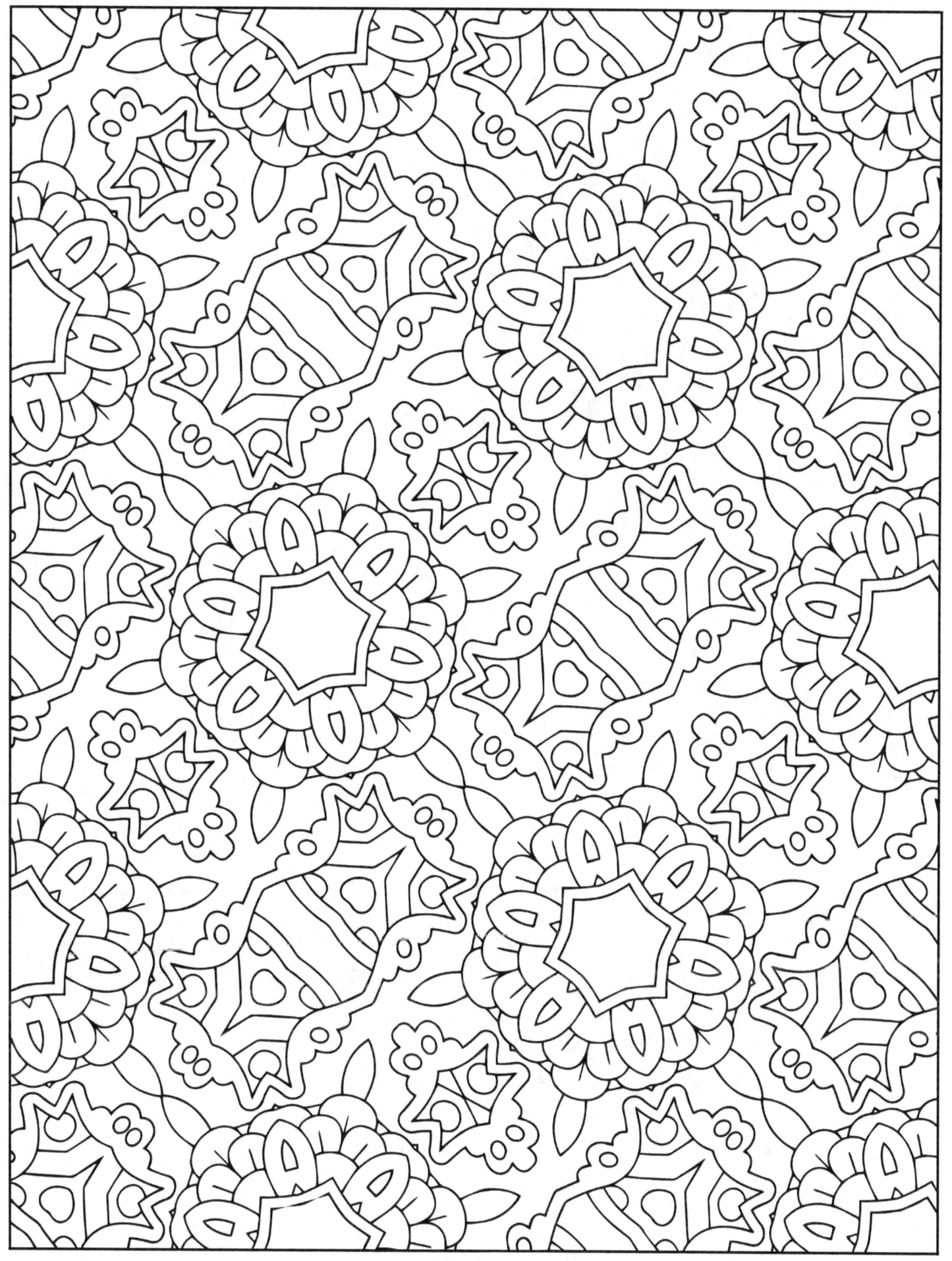

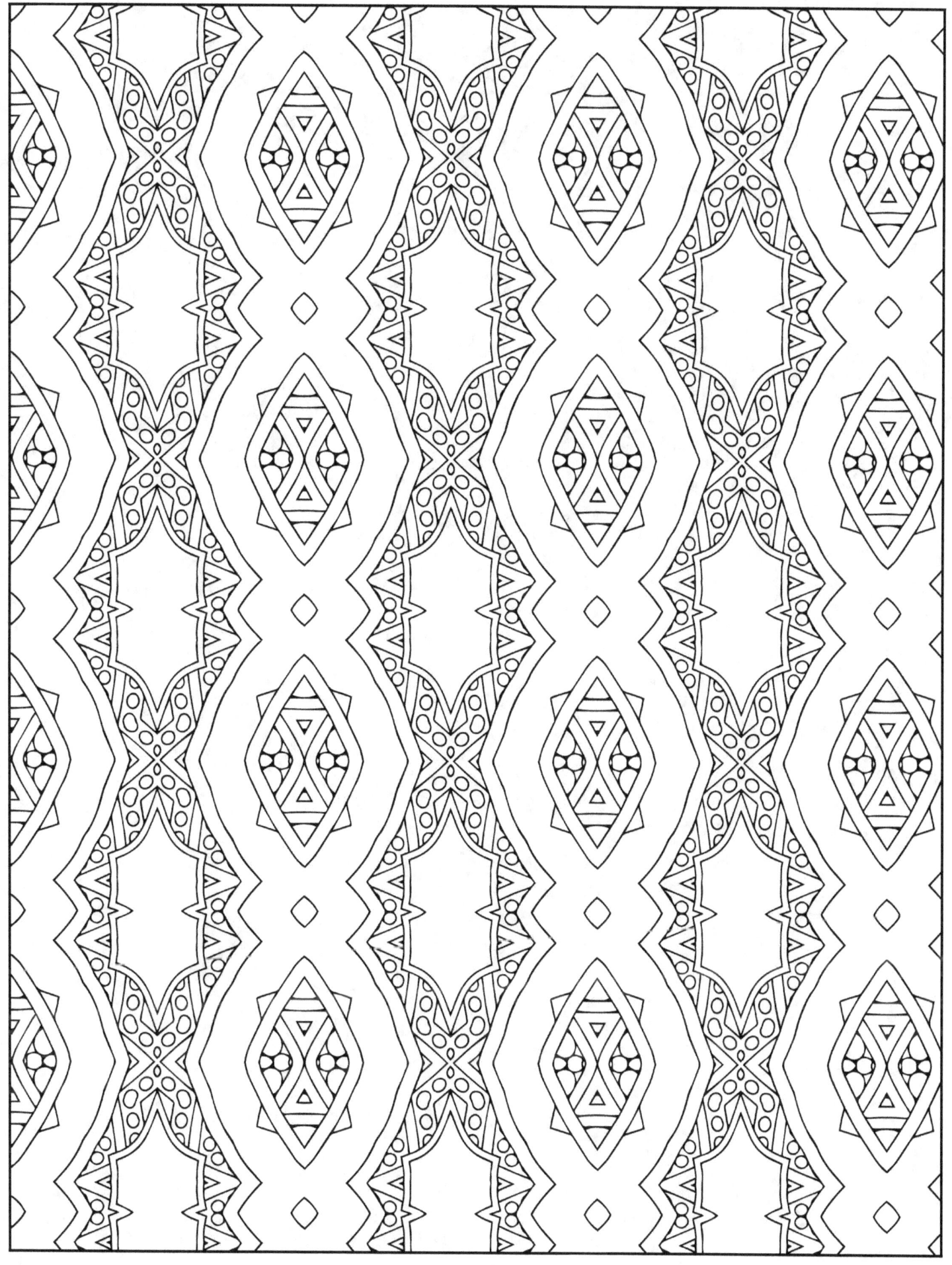

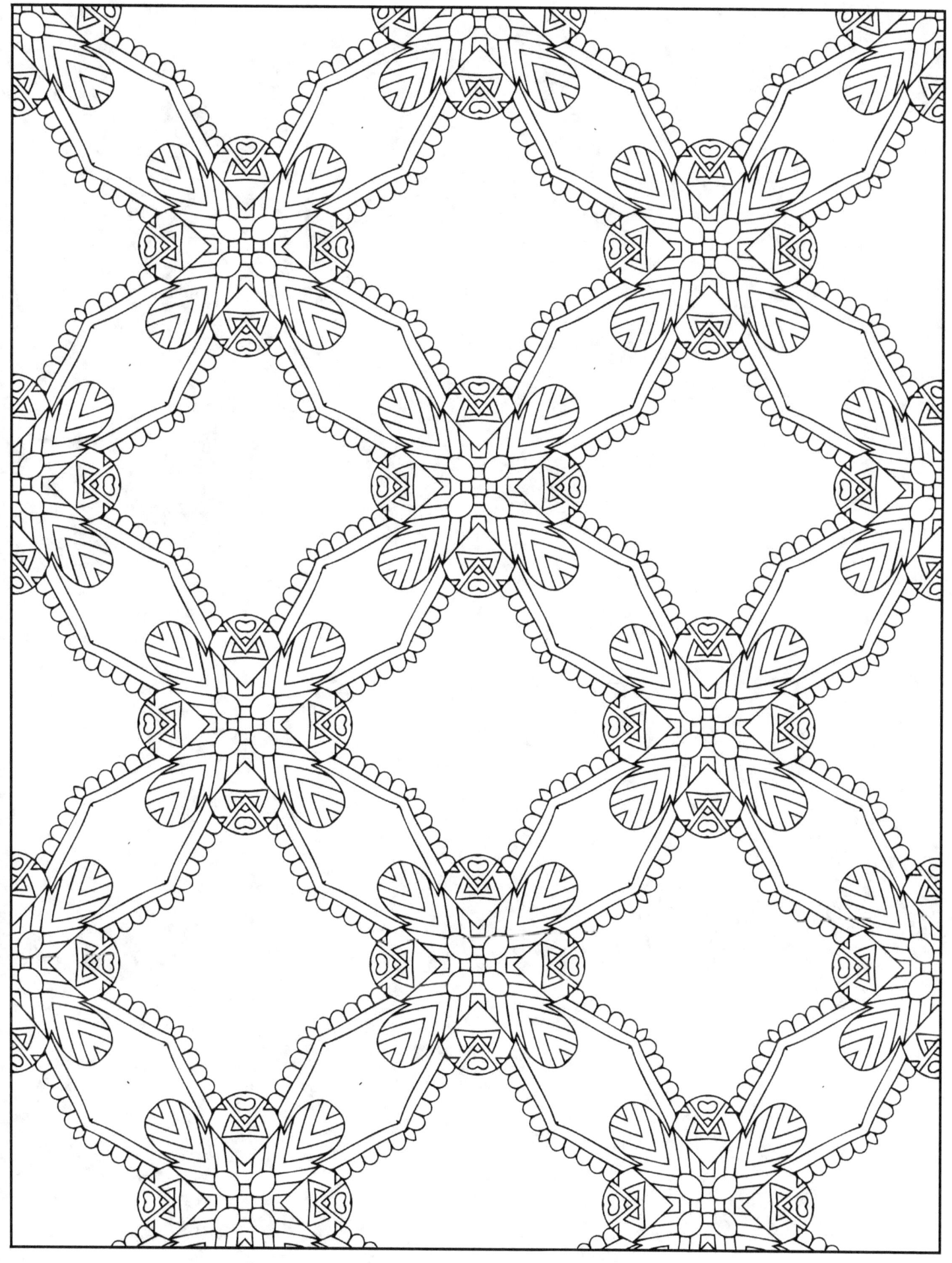

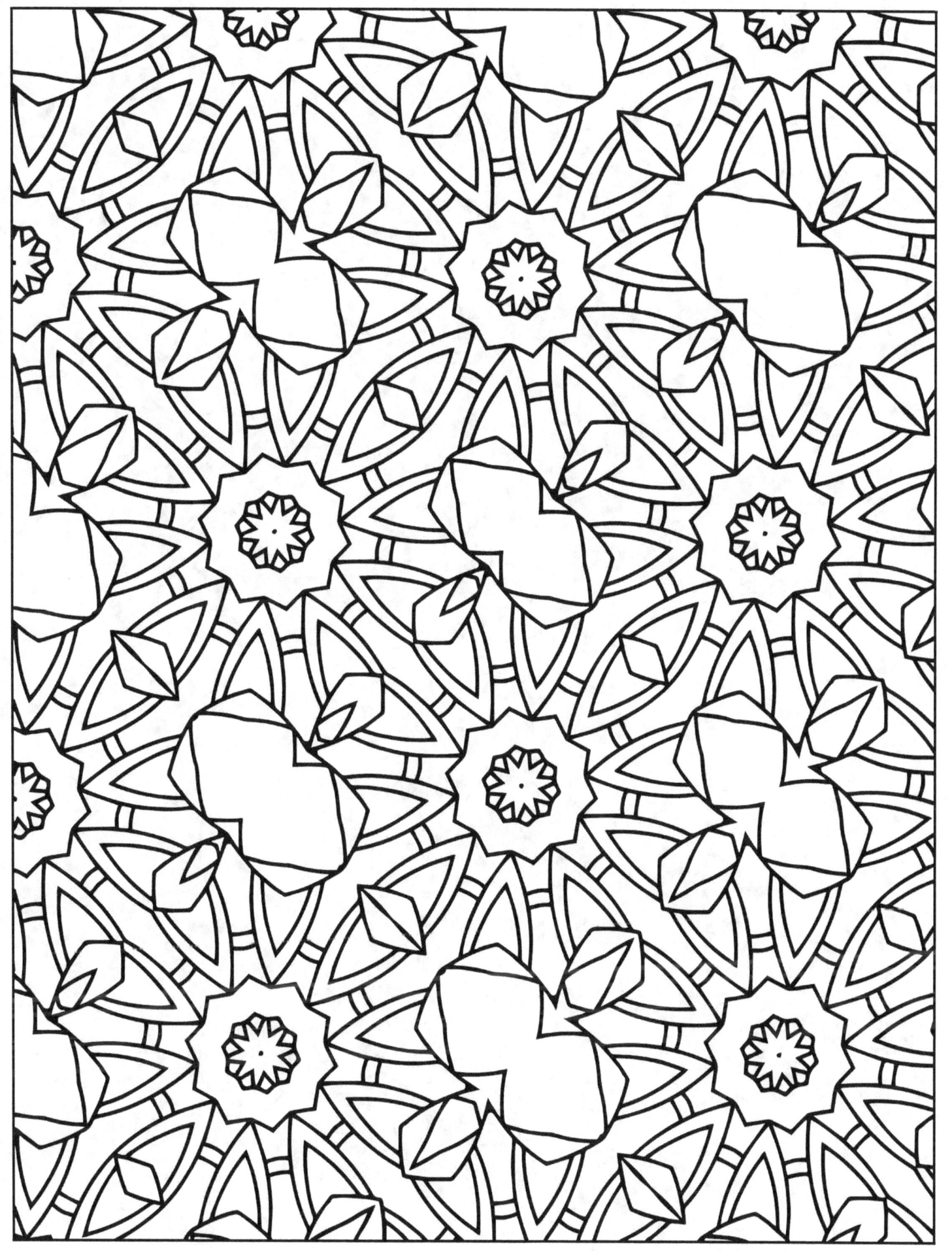

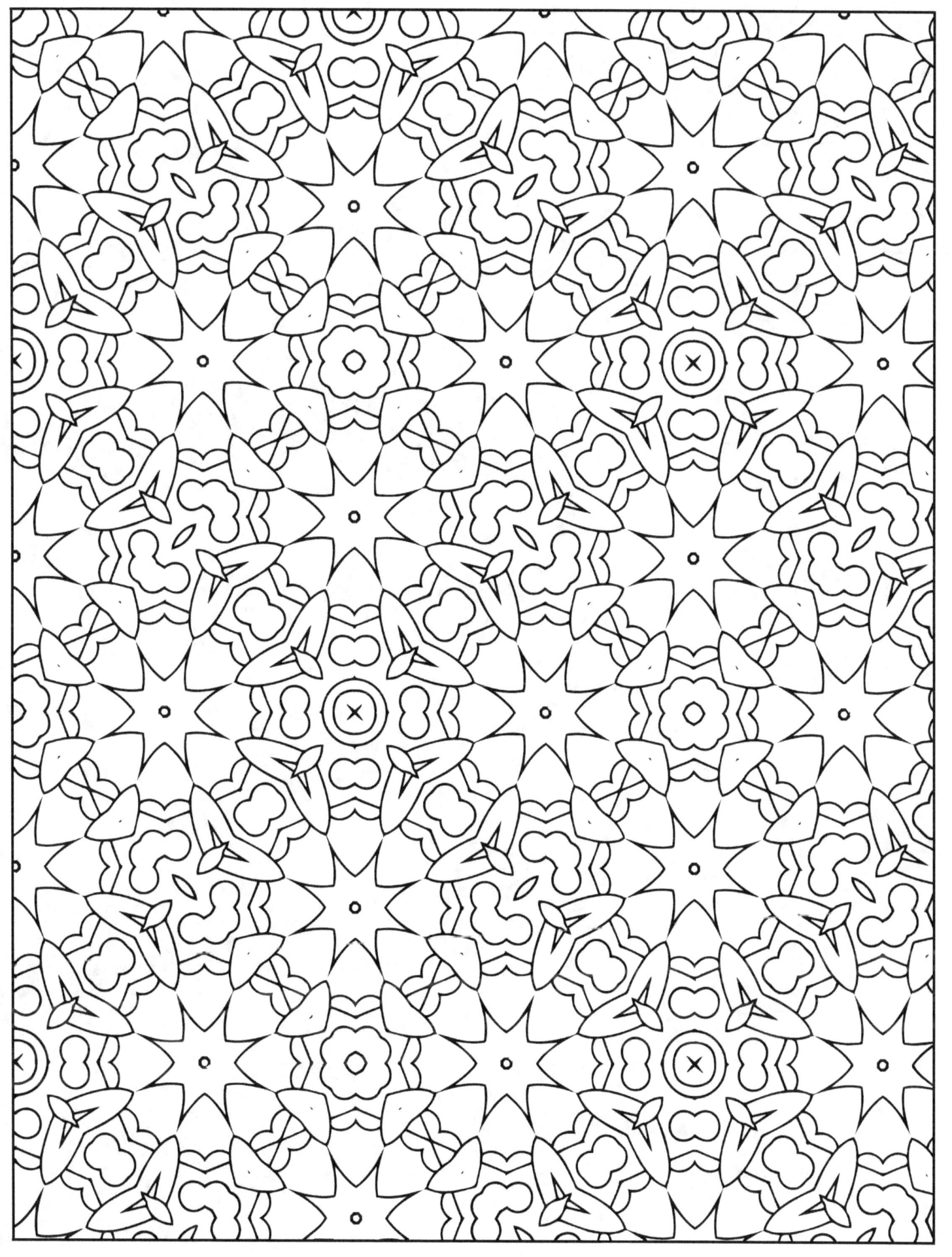

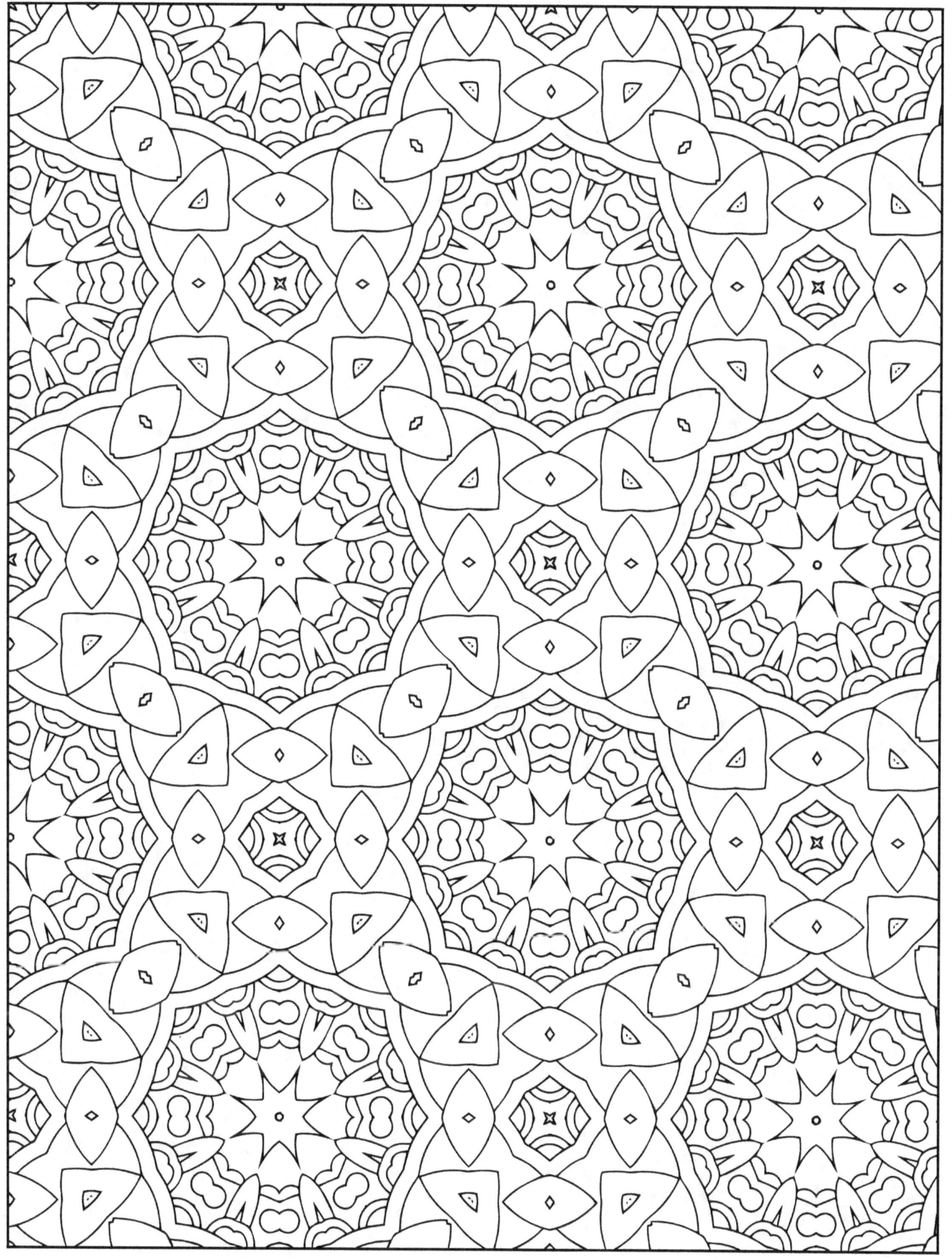

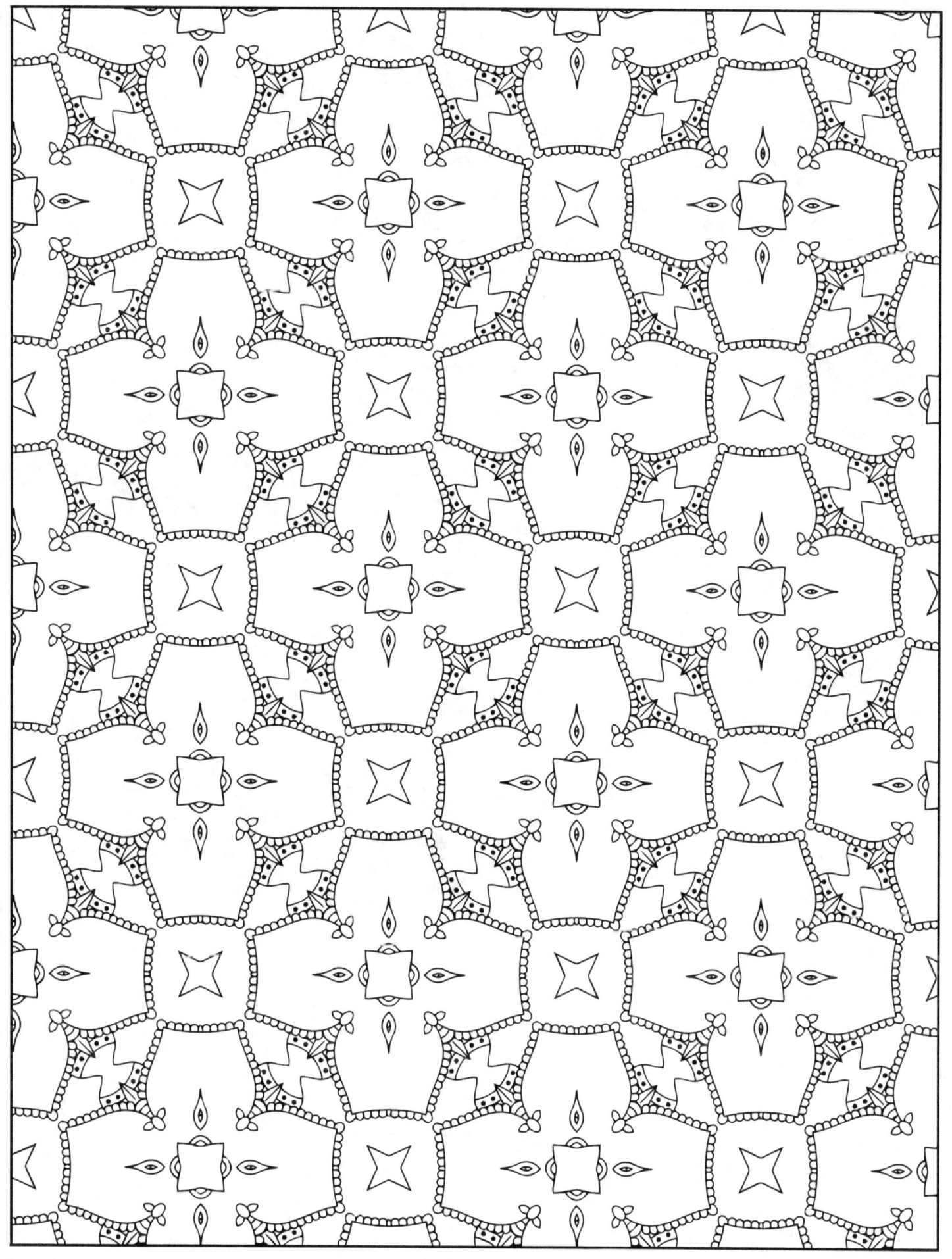

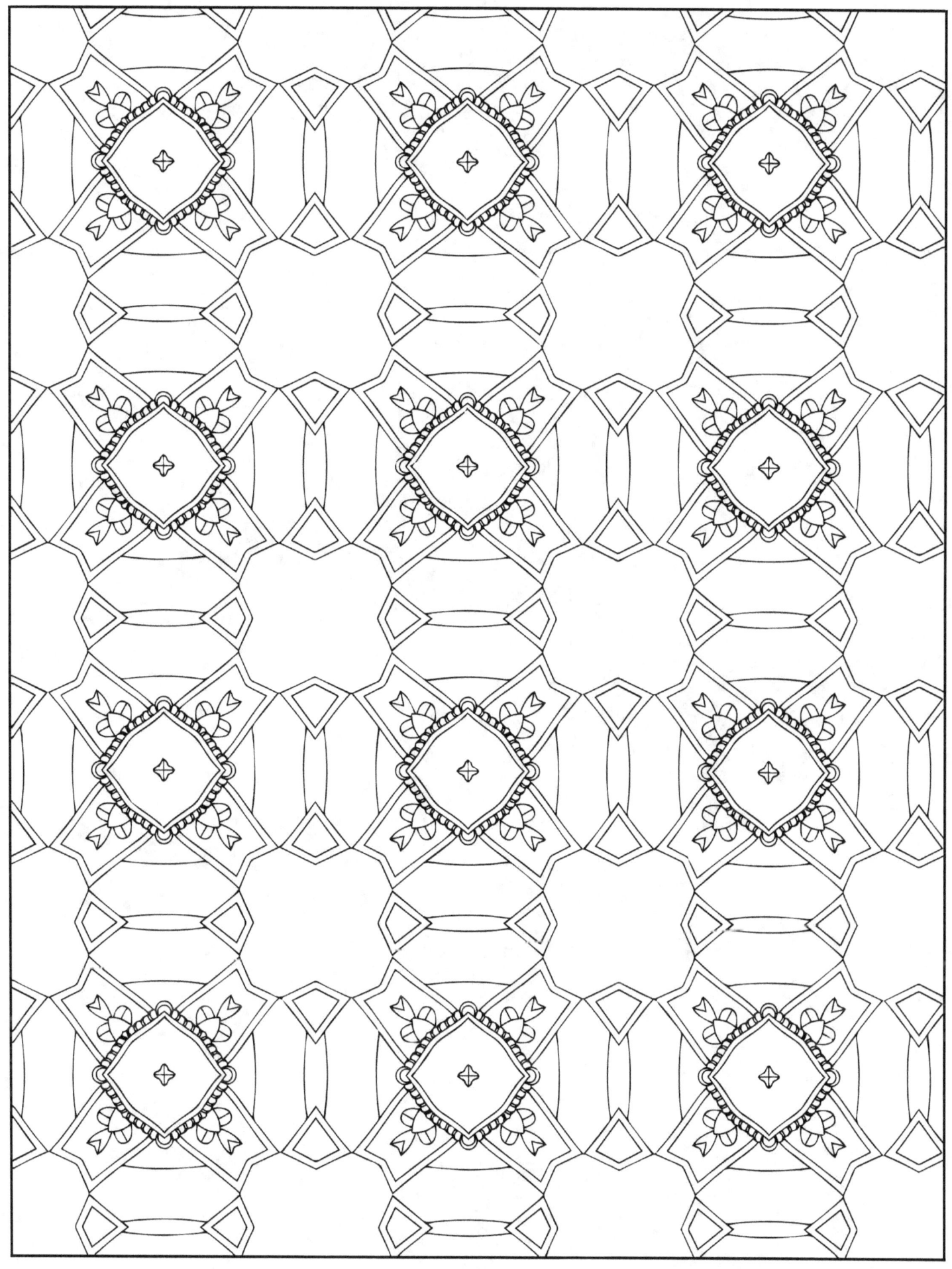

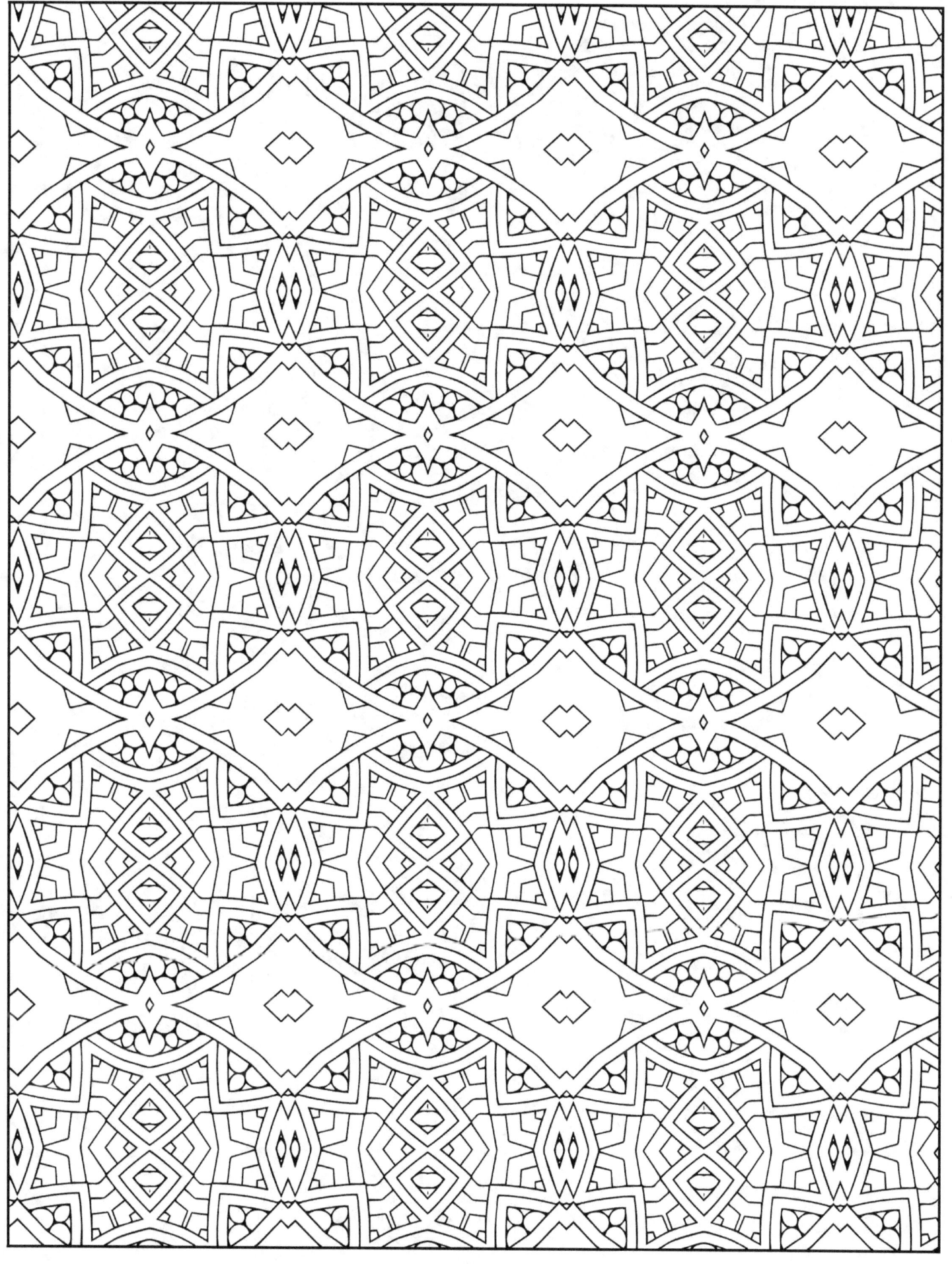

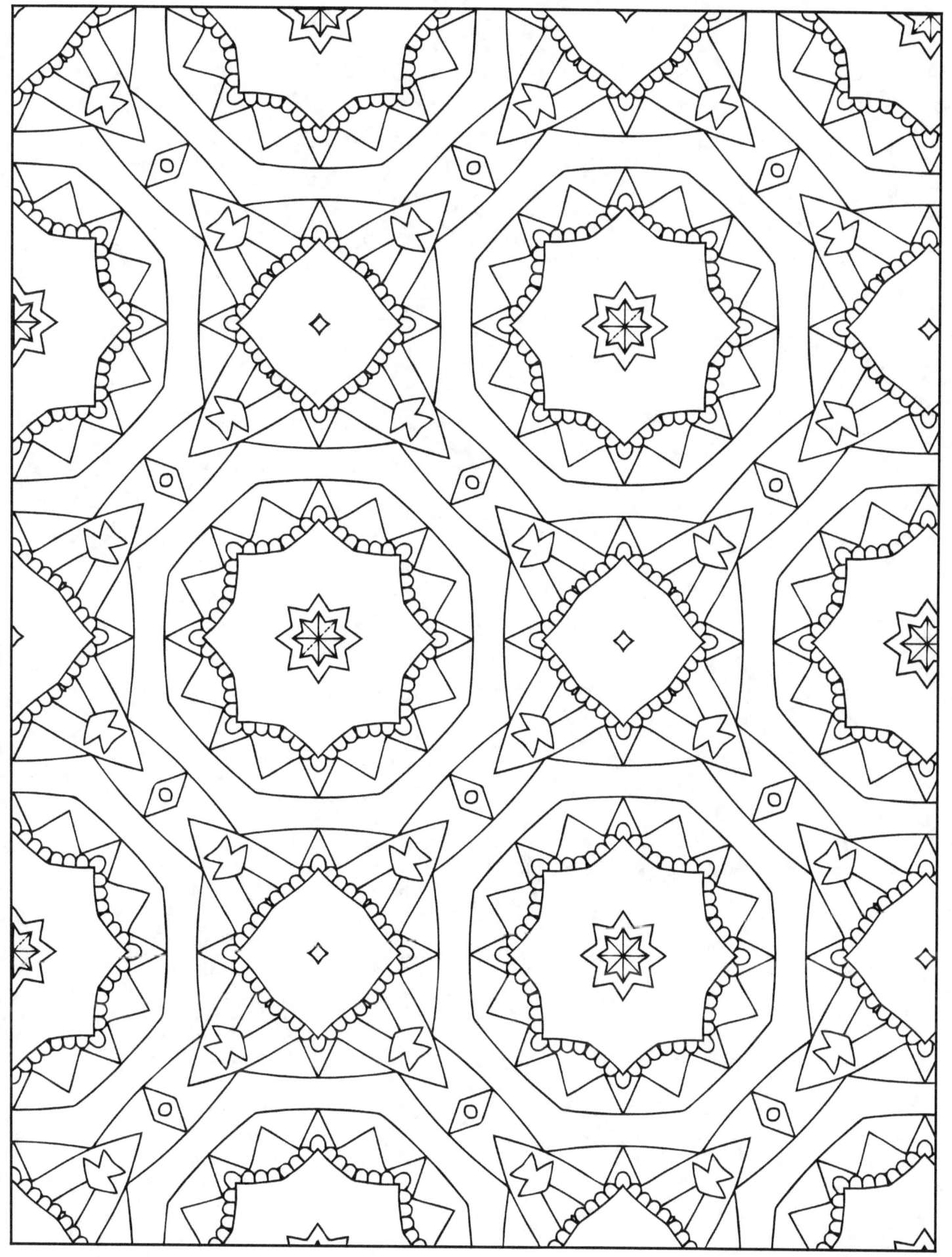

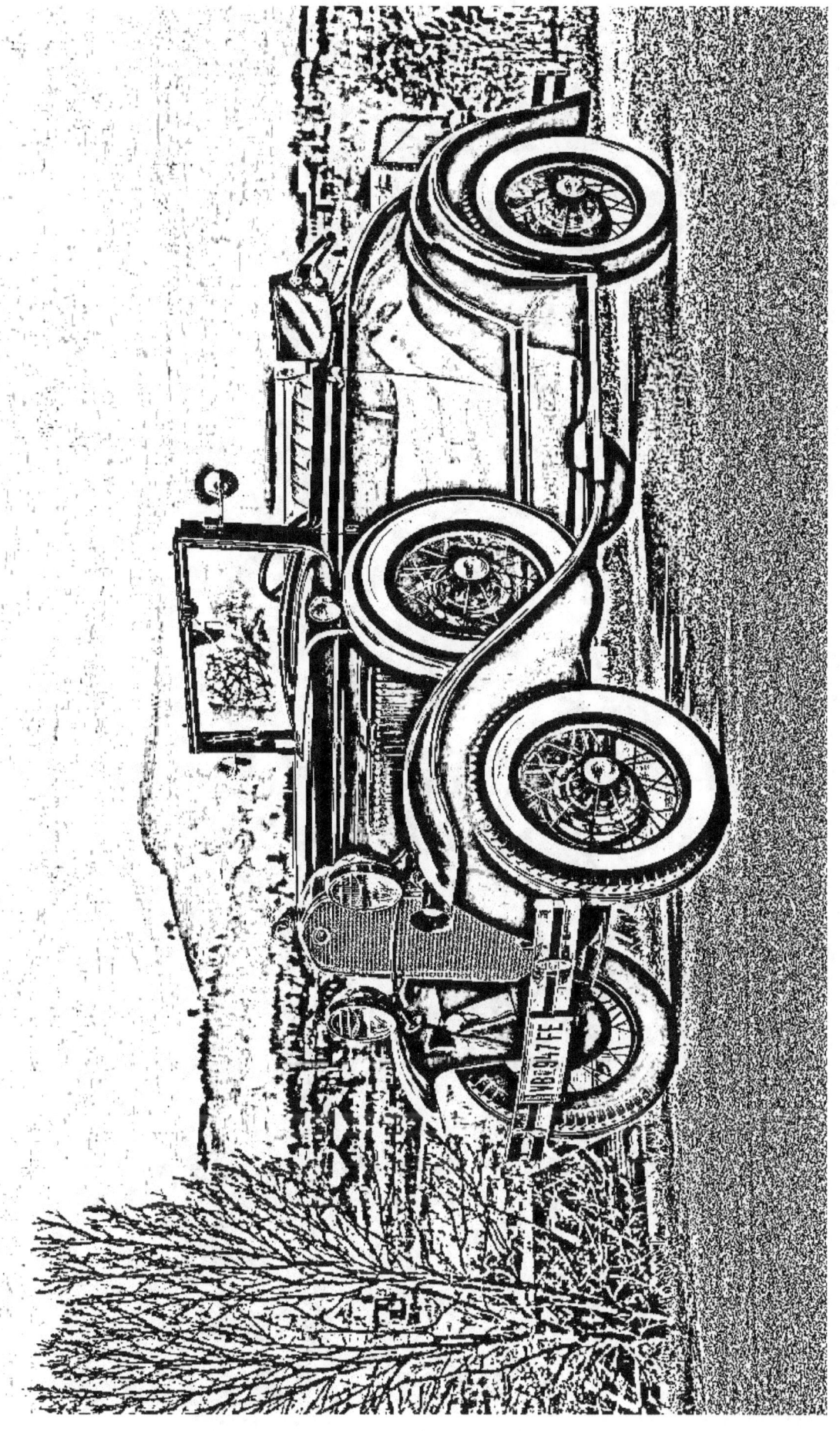

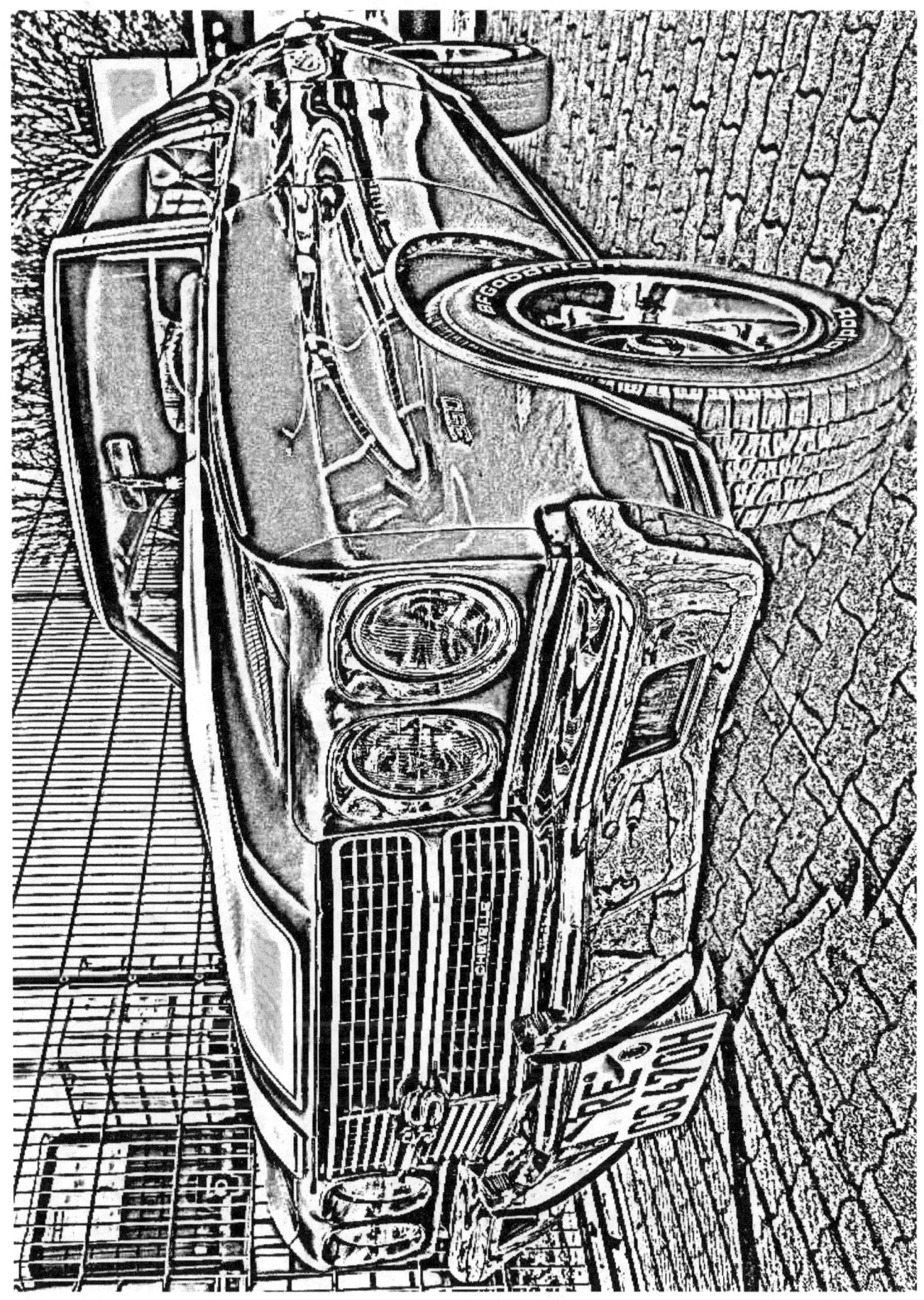

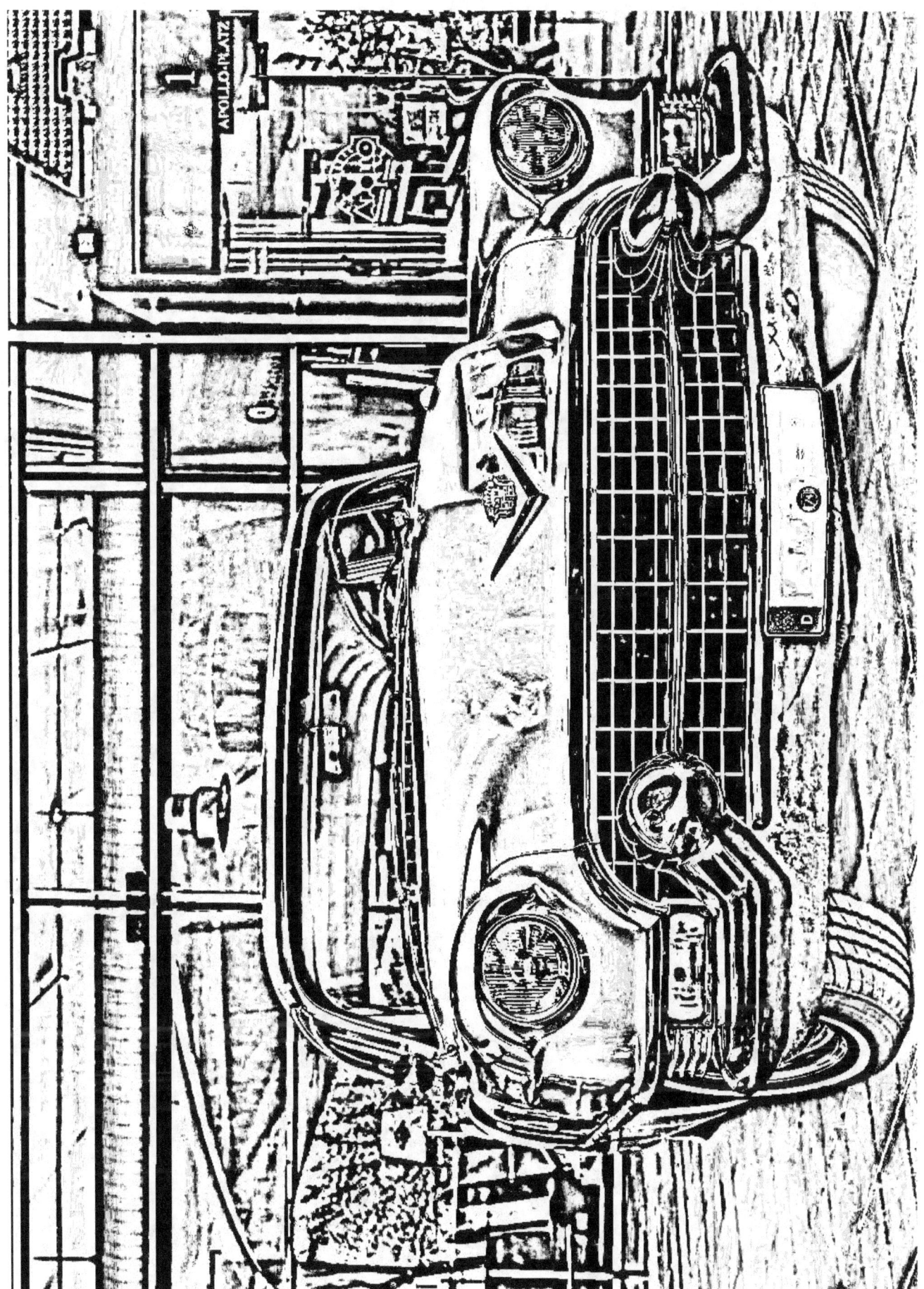

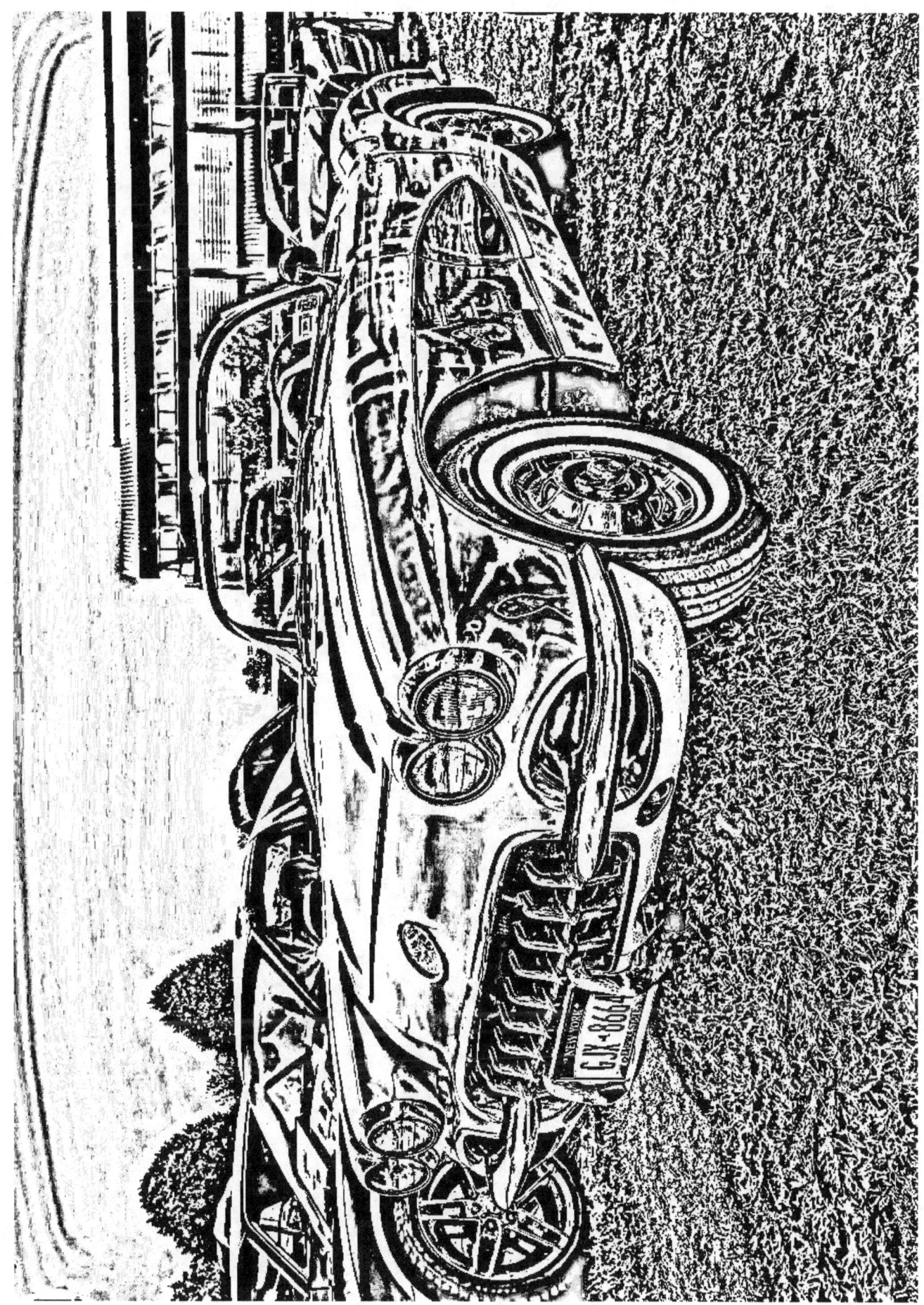

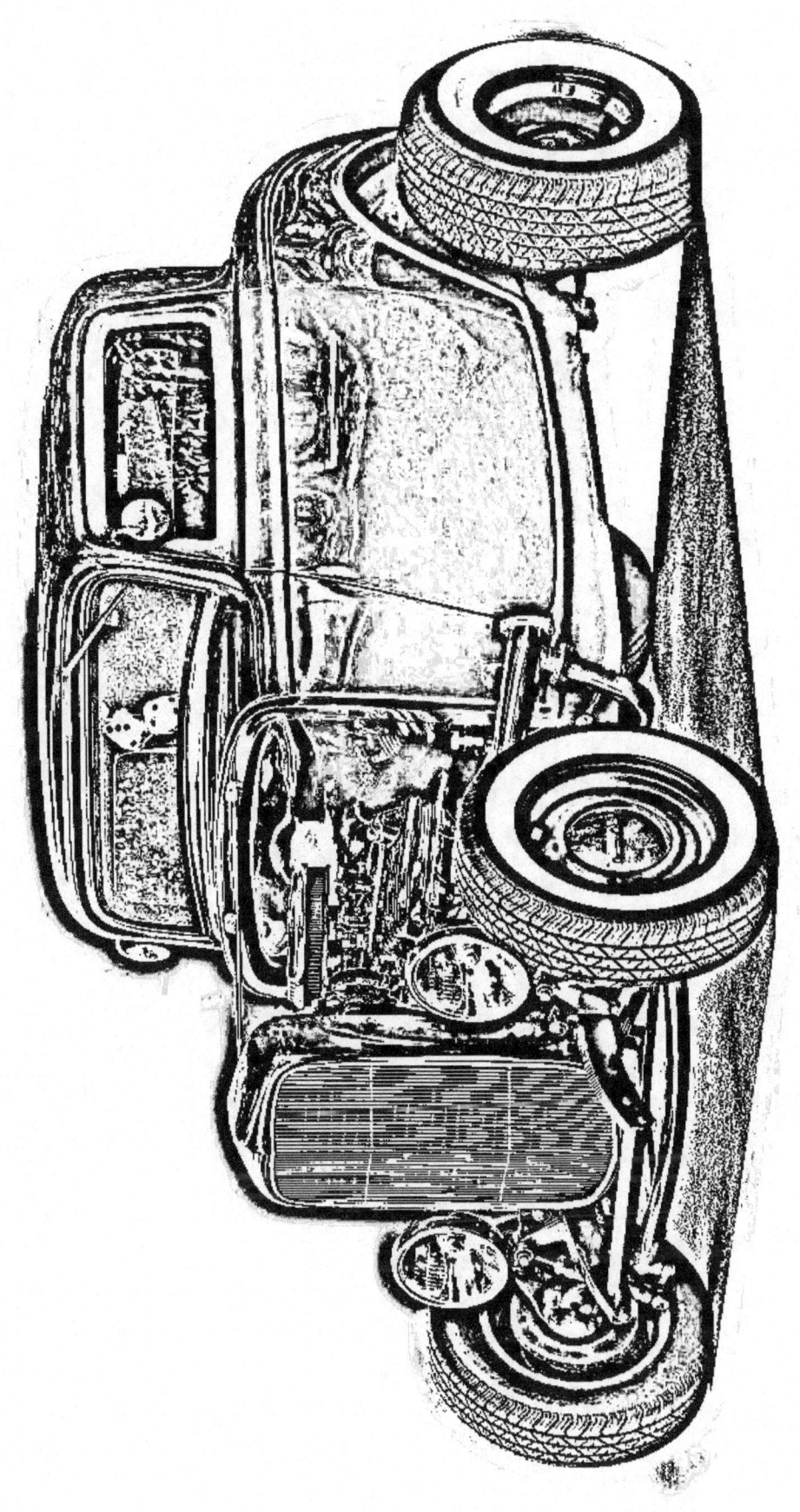

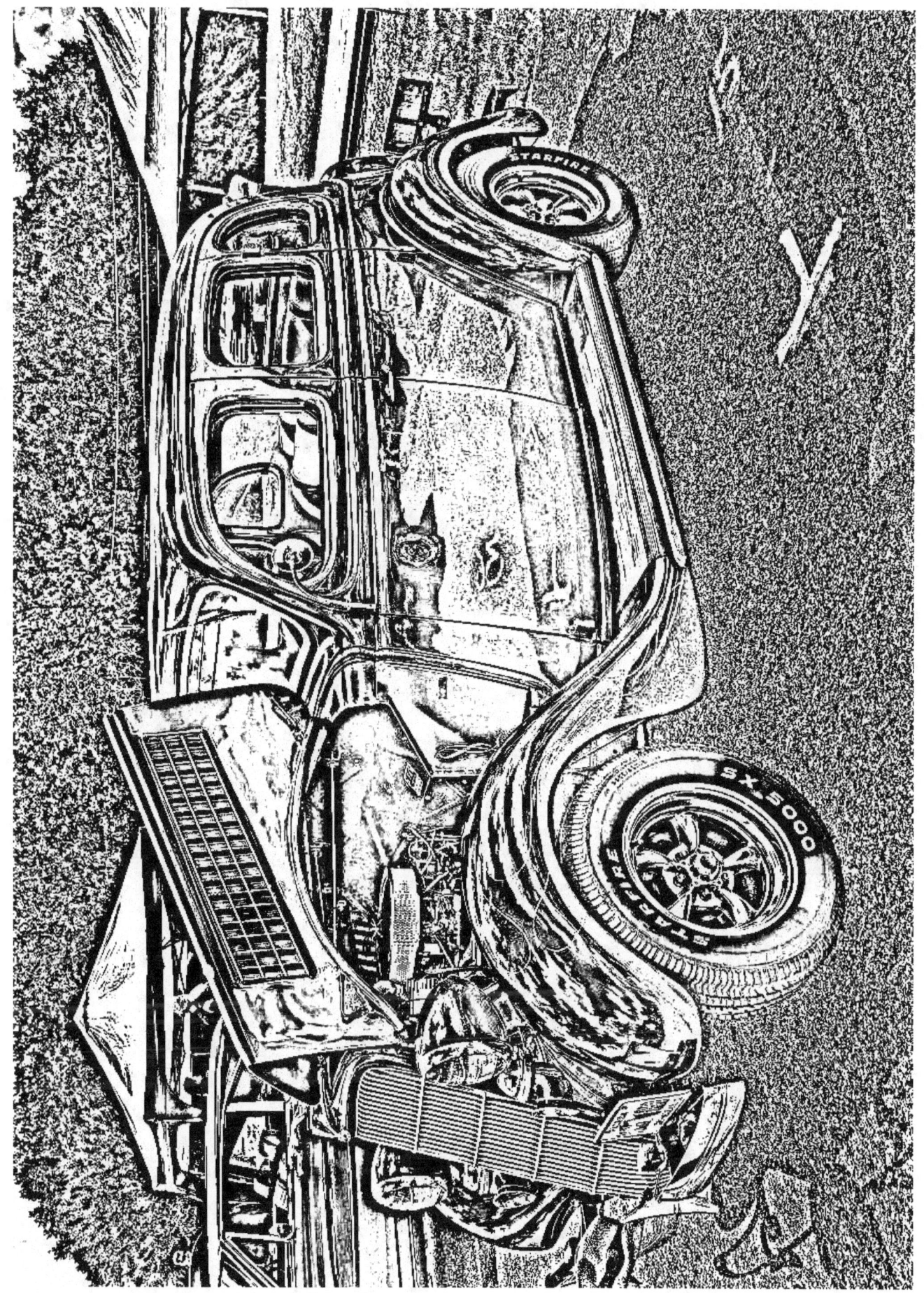

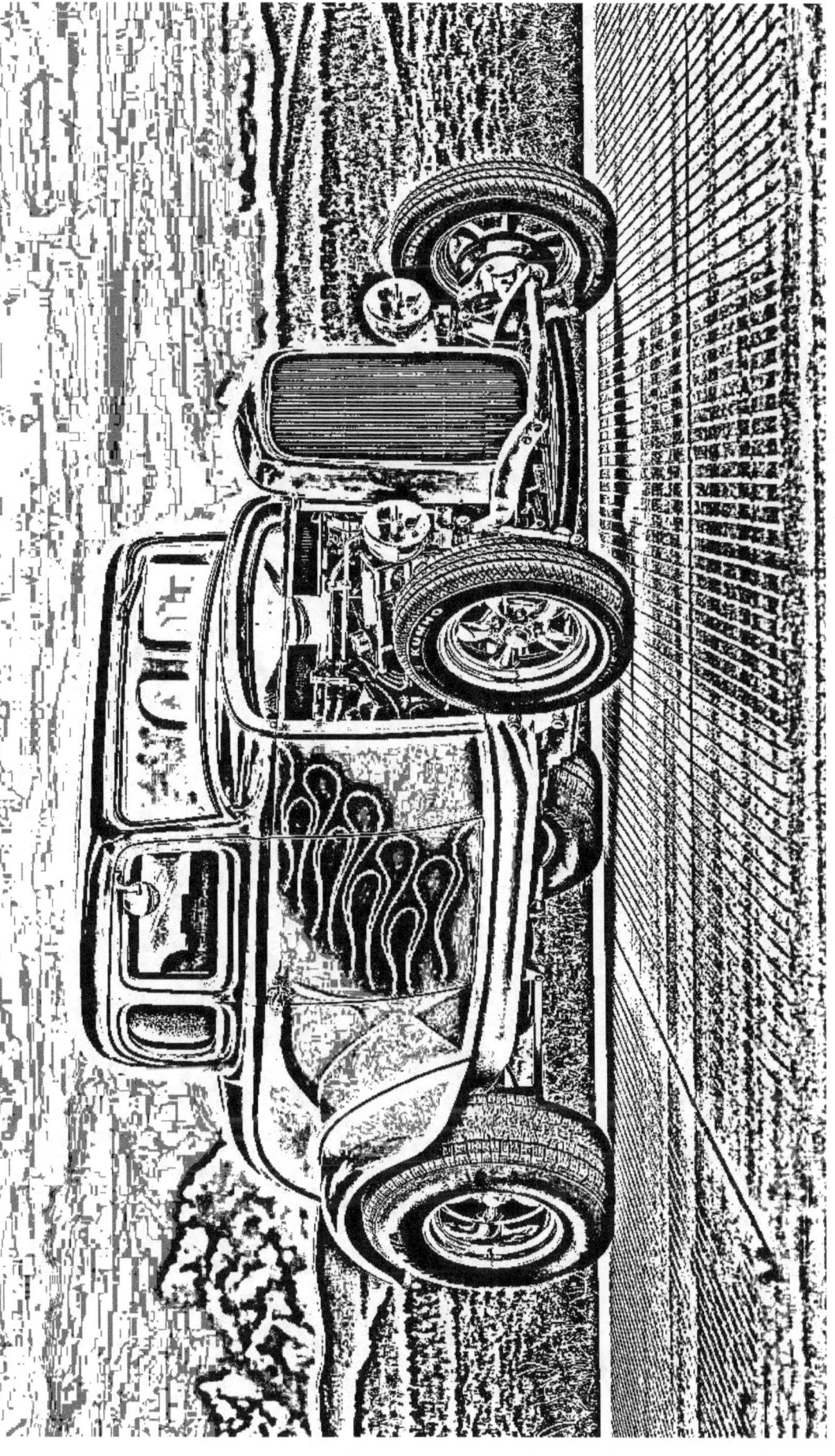

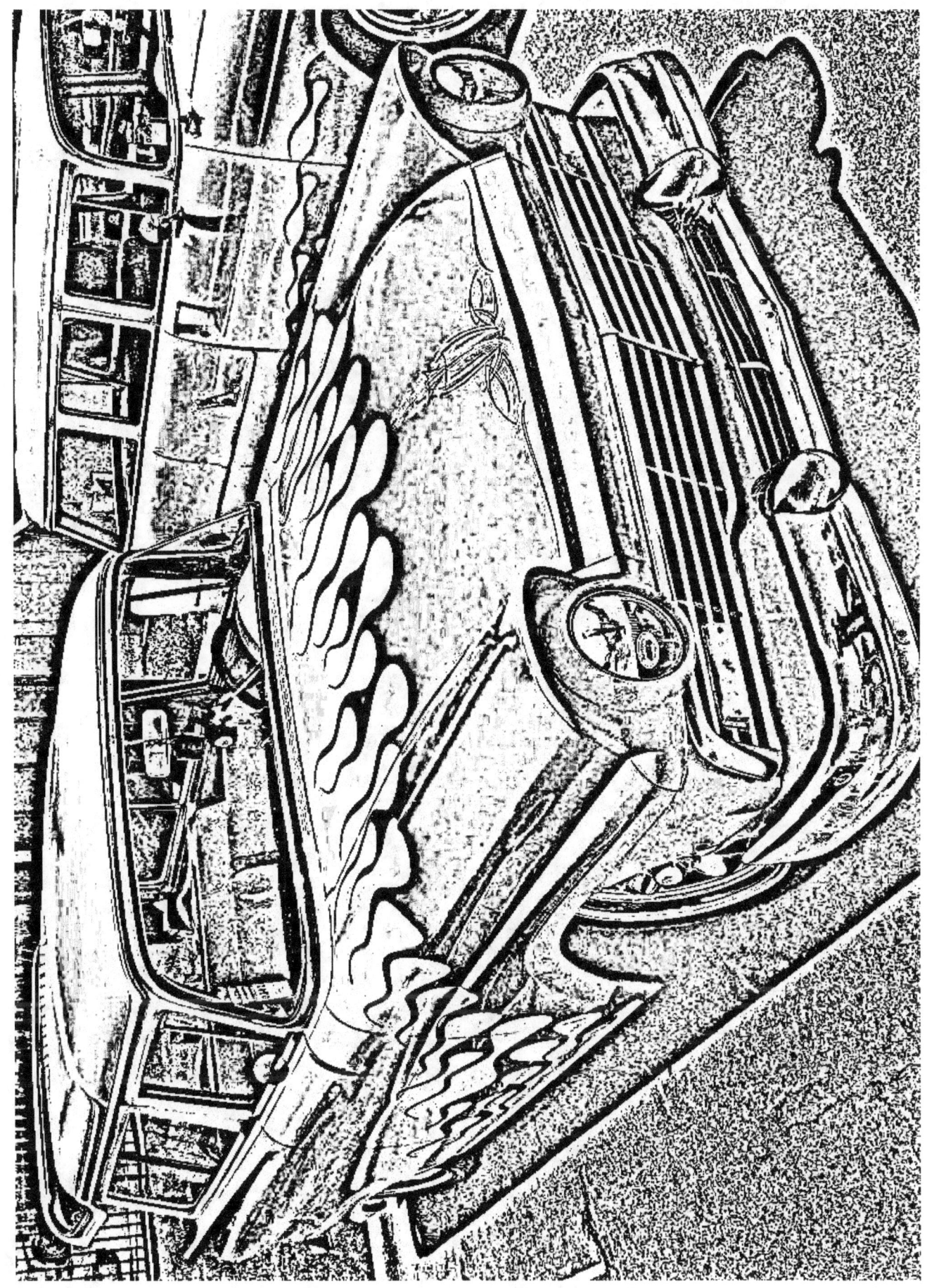

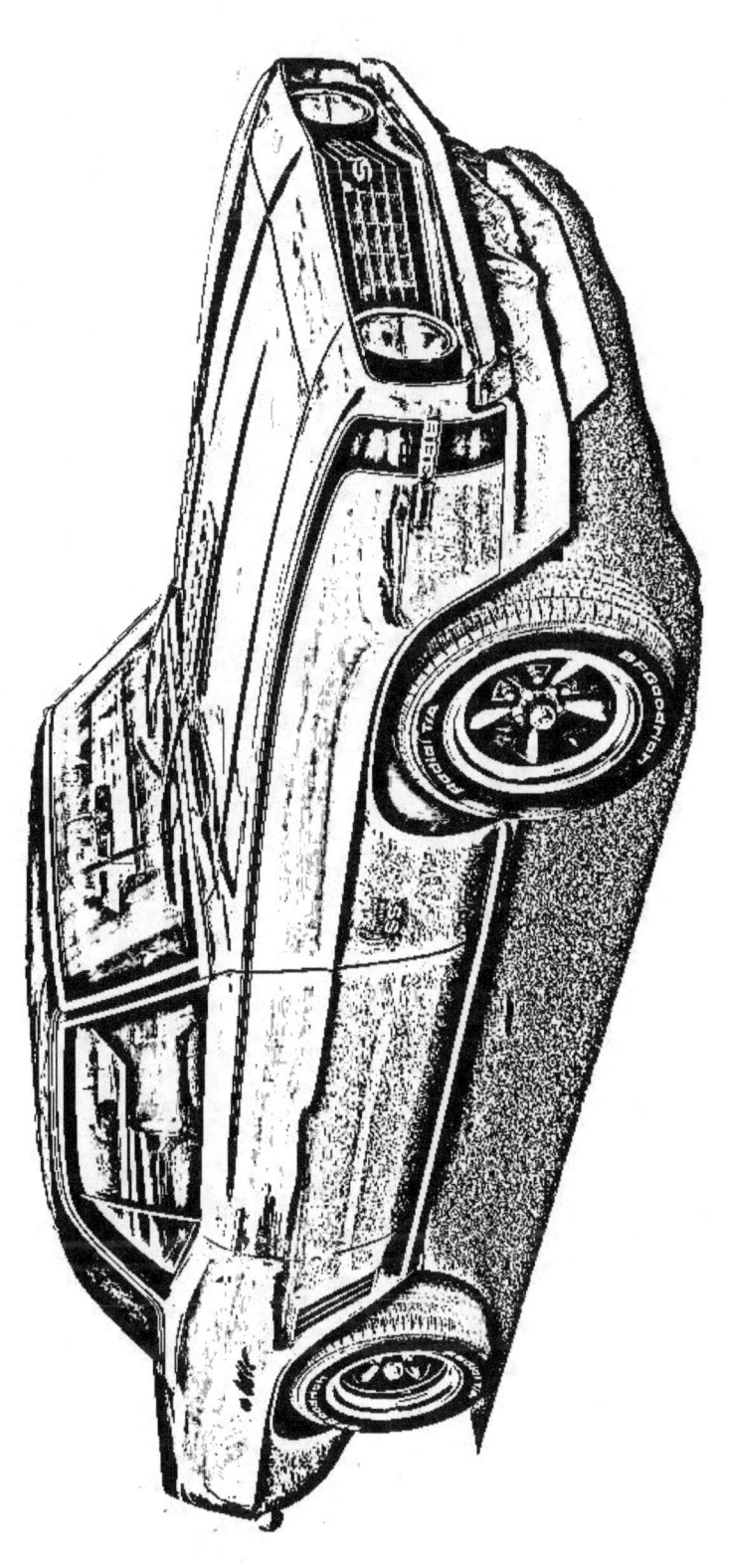

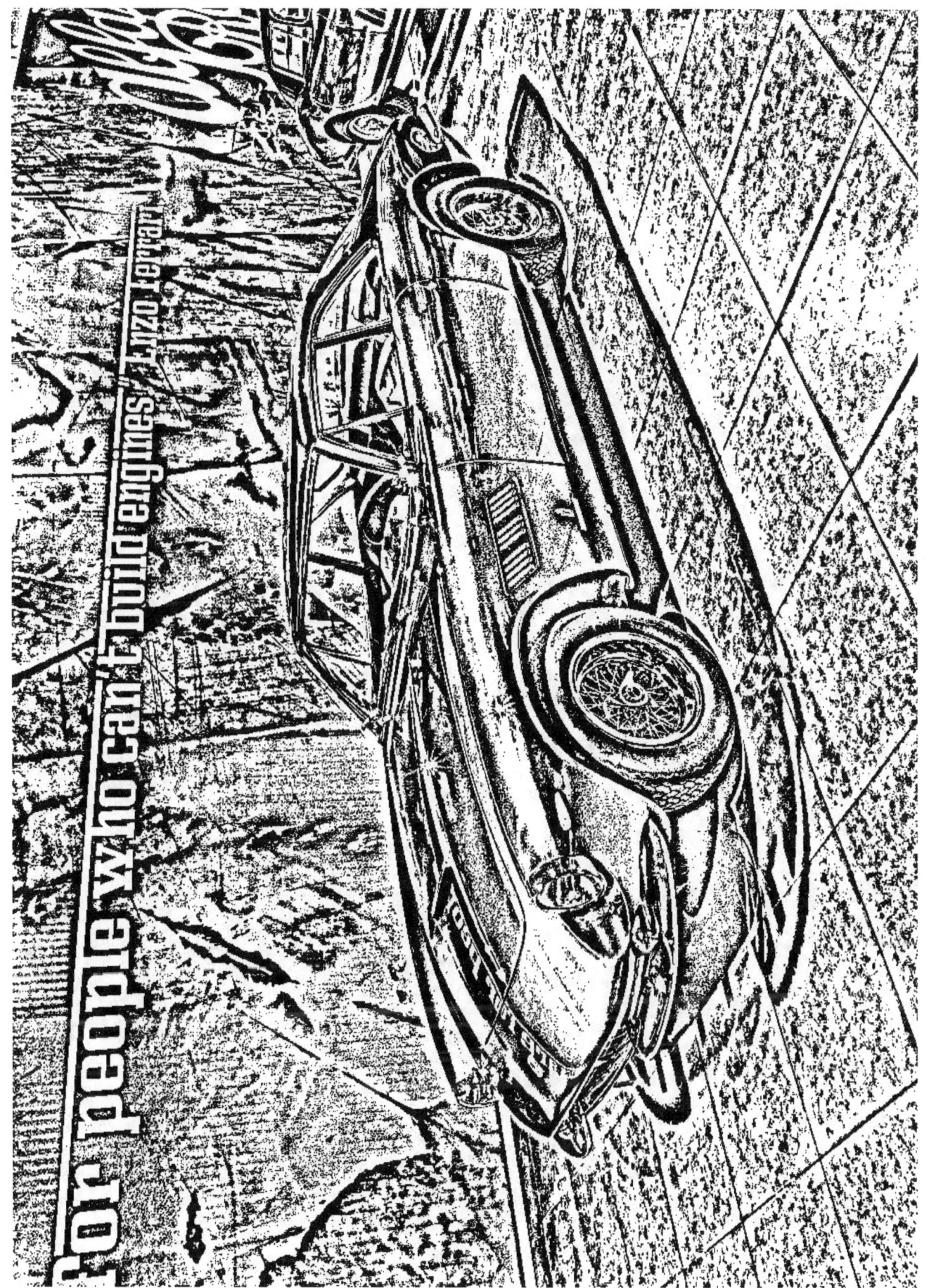

for people who can't build engines. Enzo Ferrari

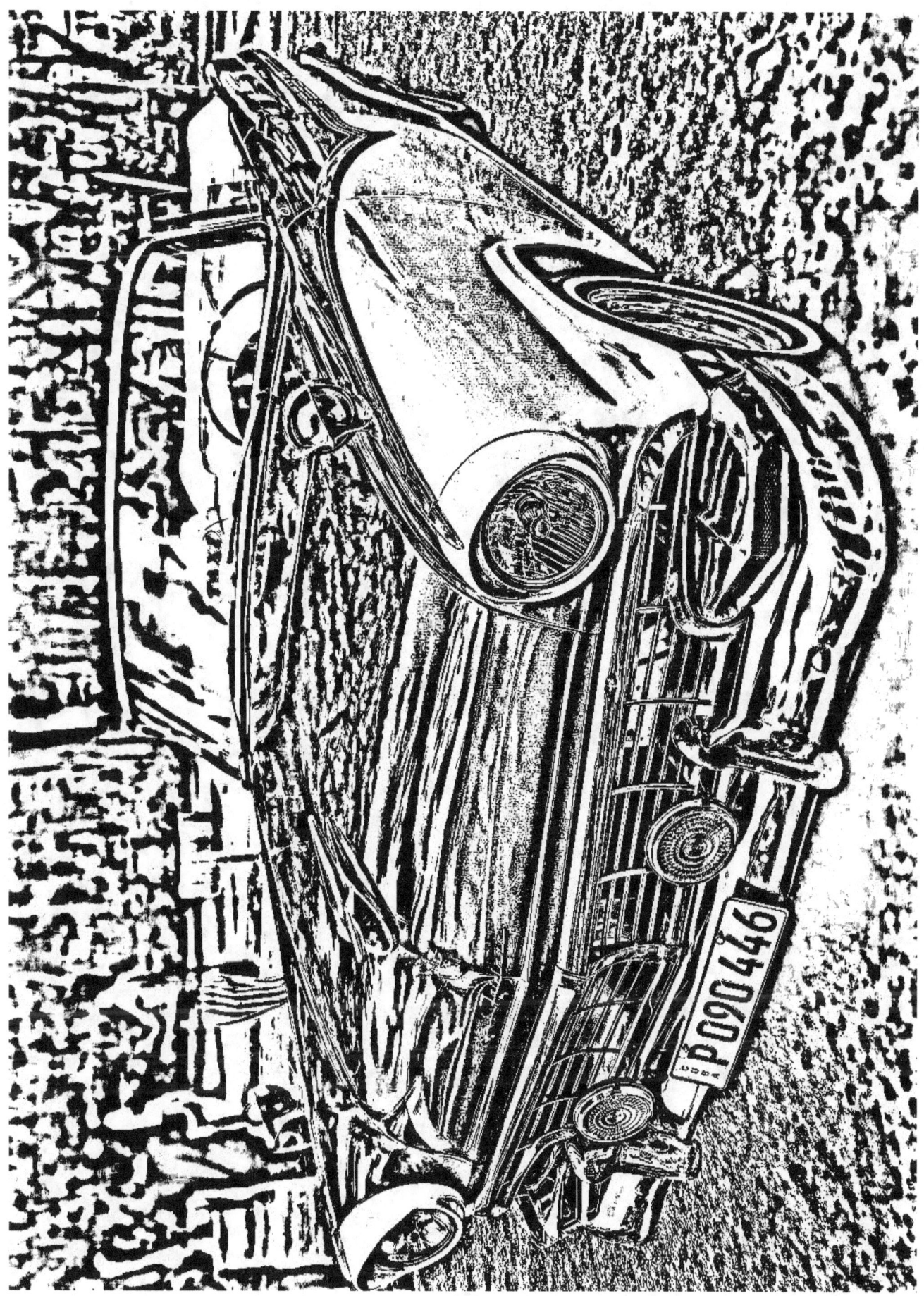

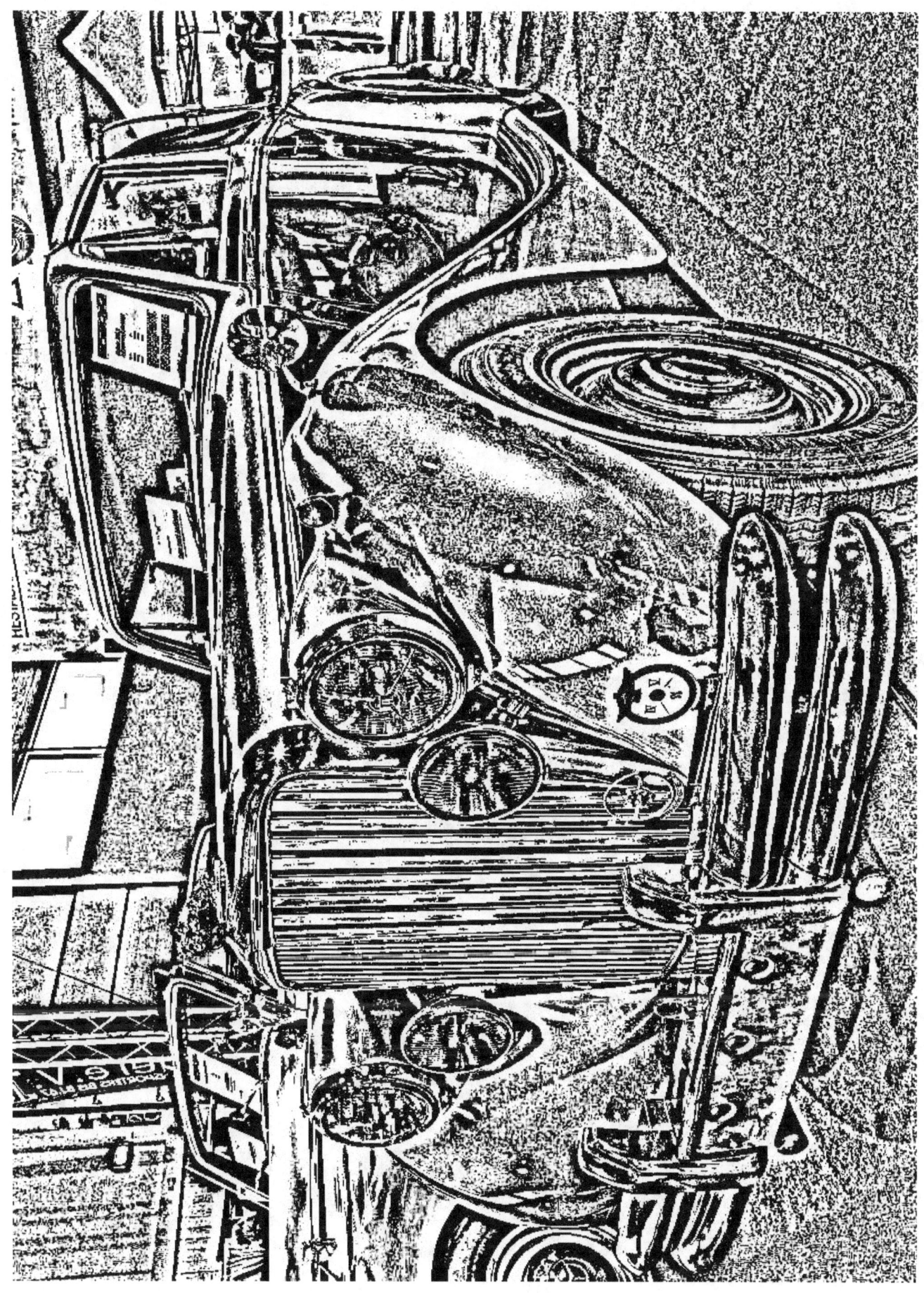

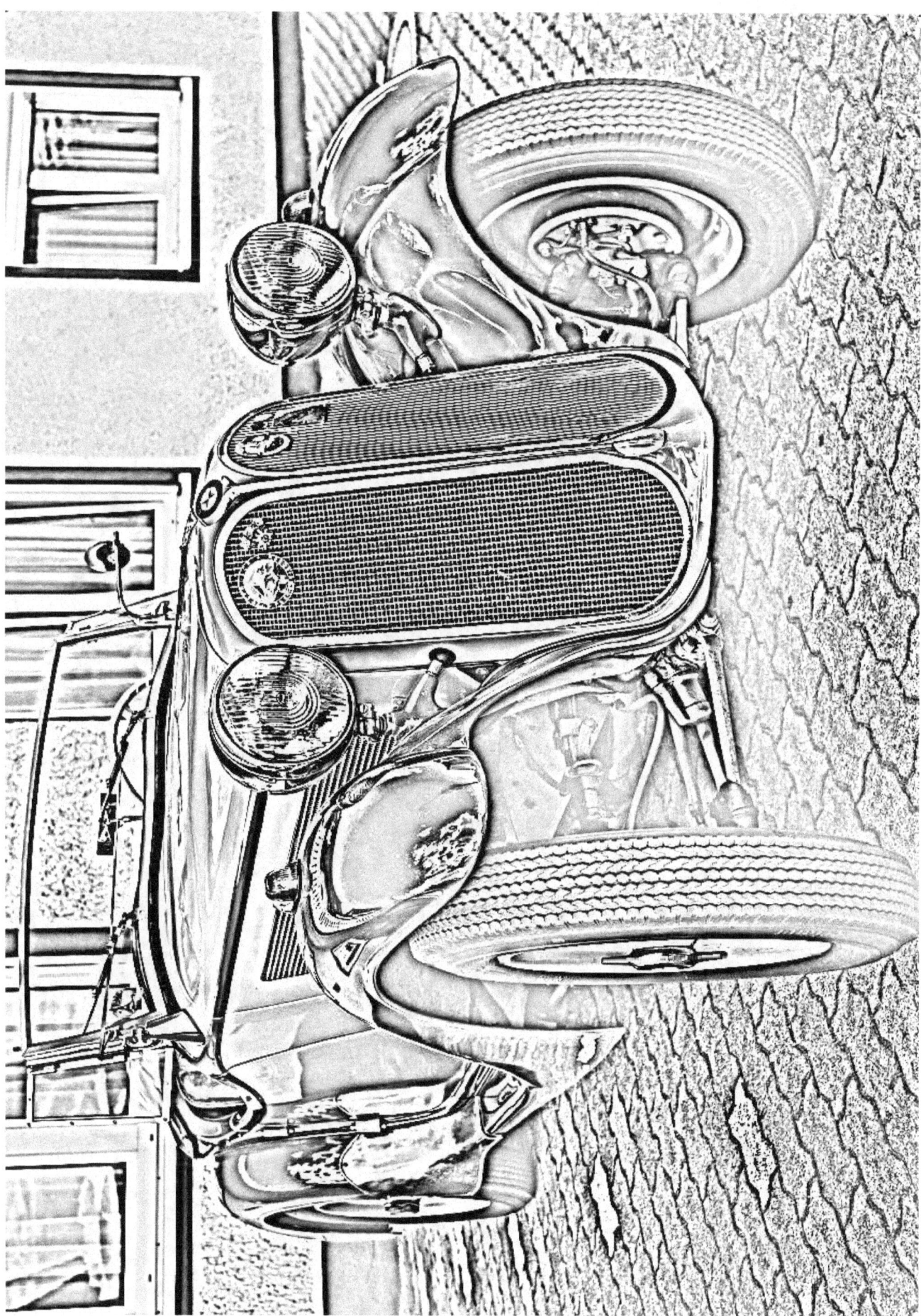

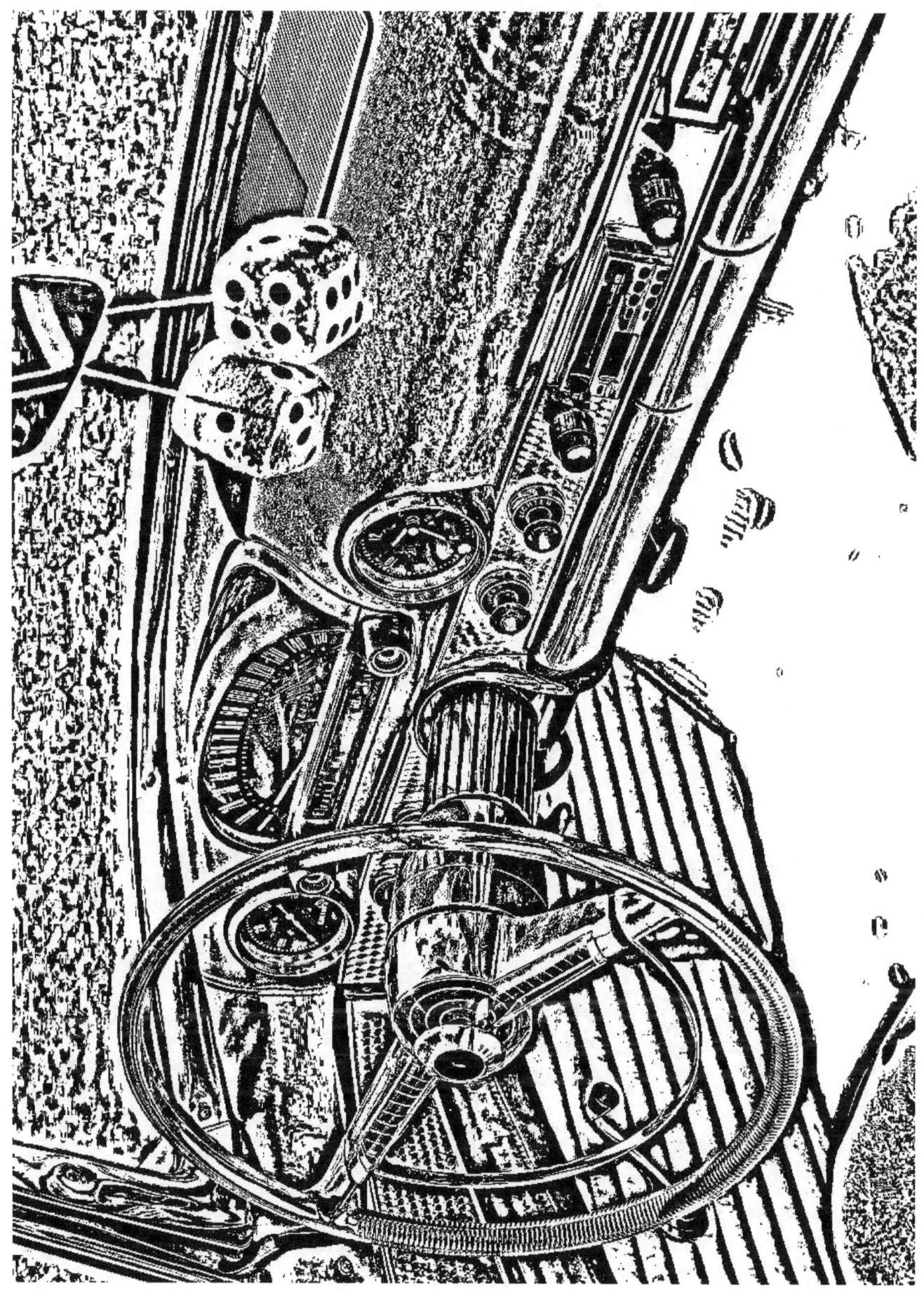

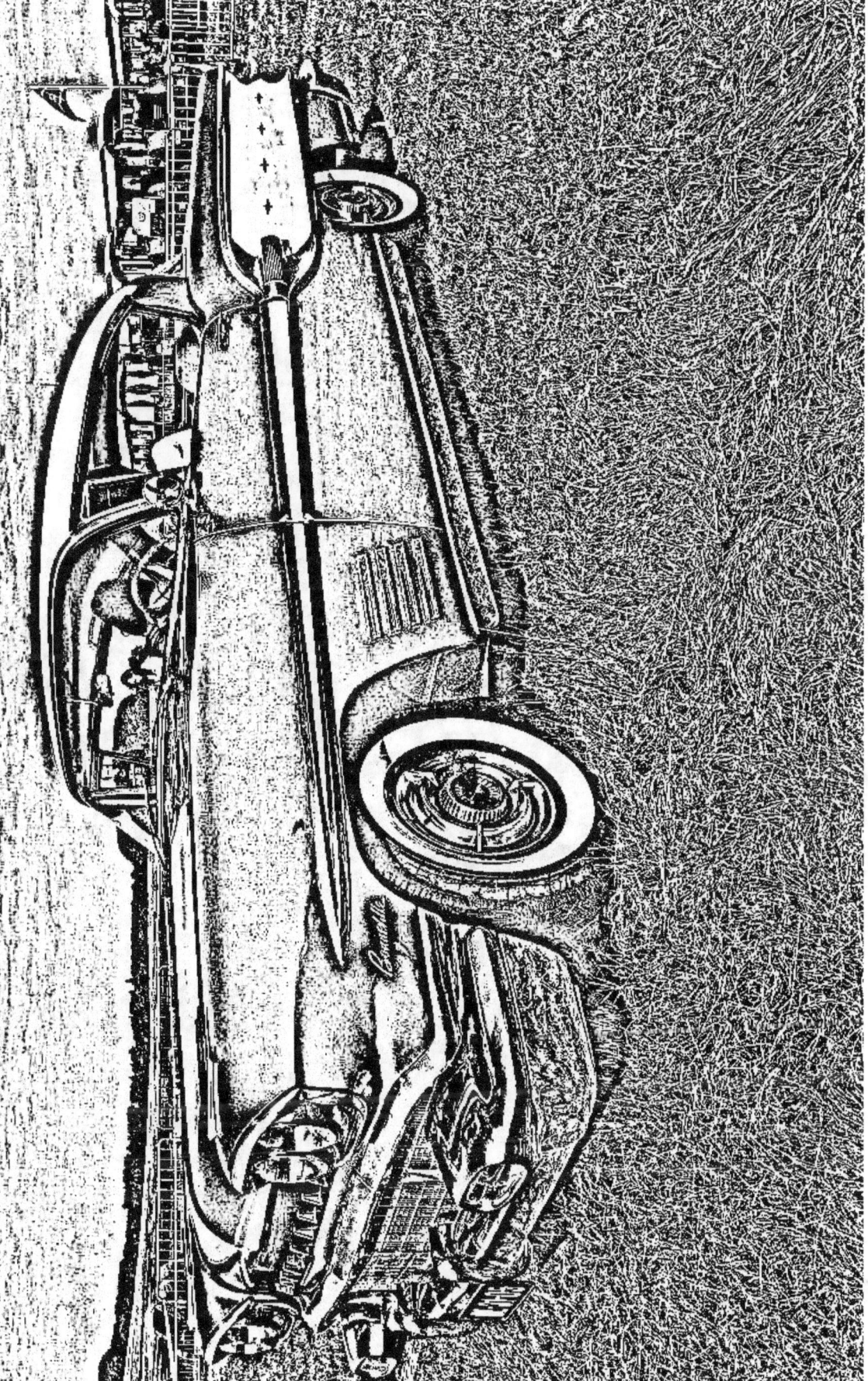

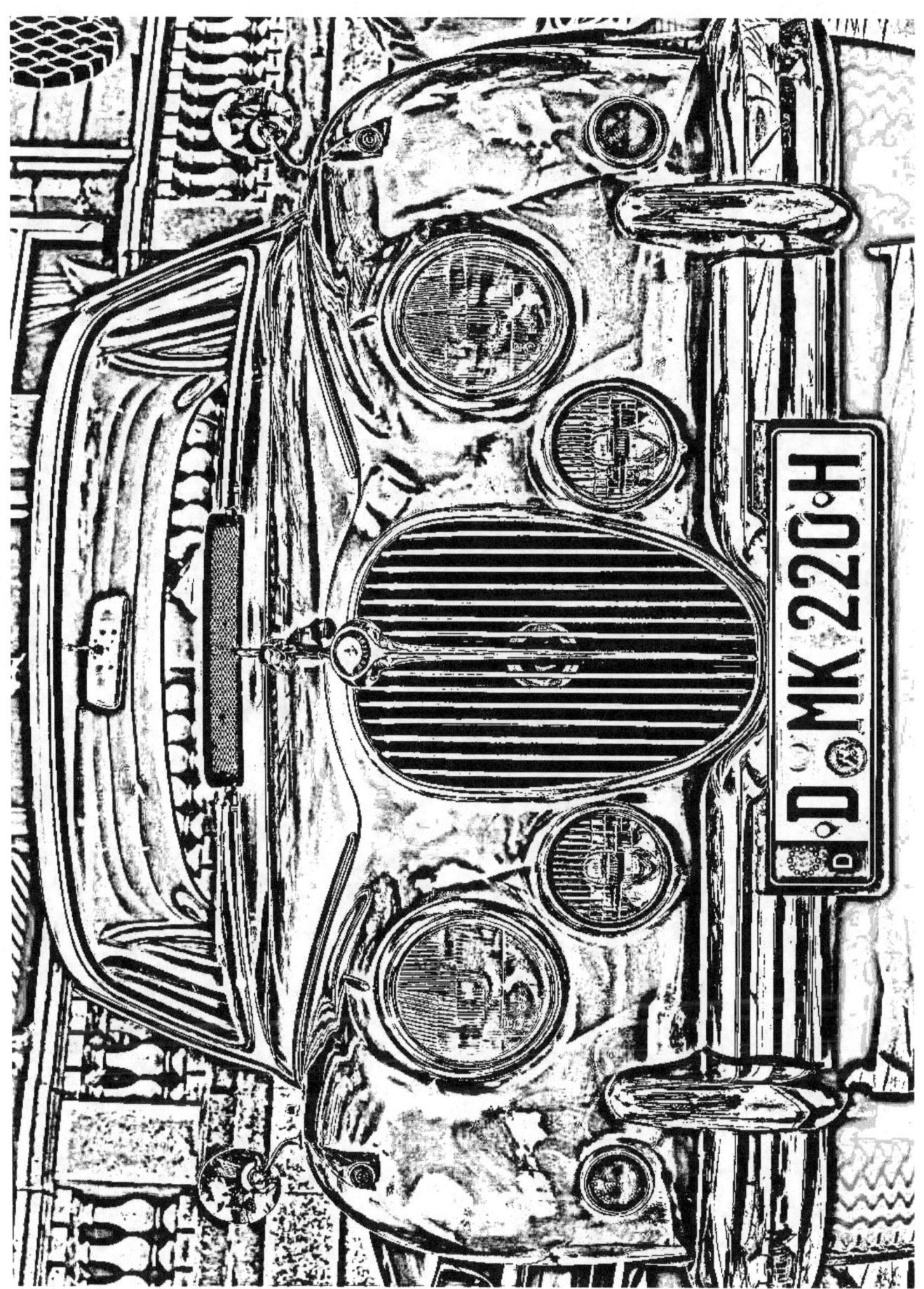

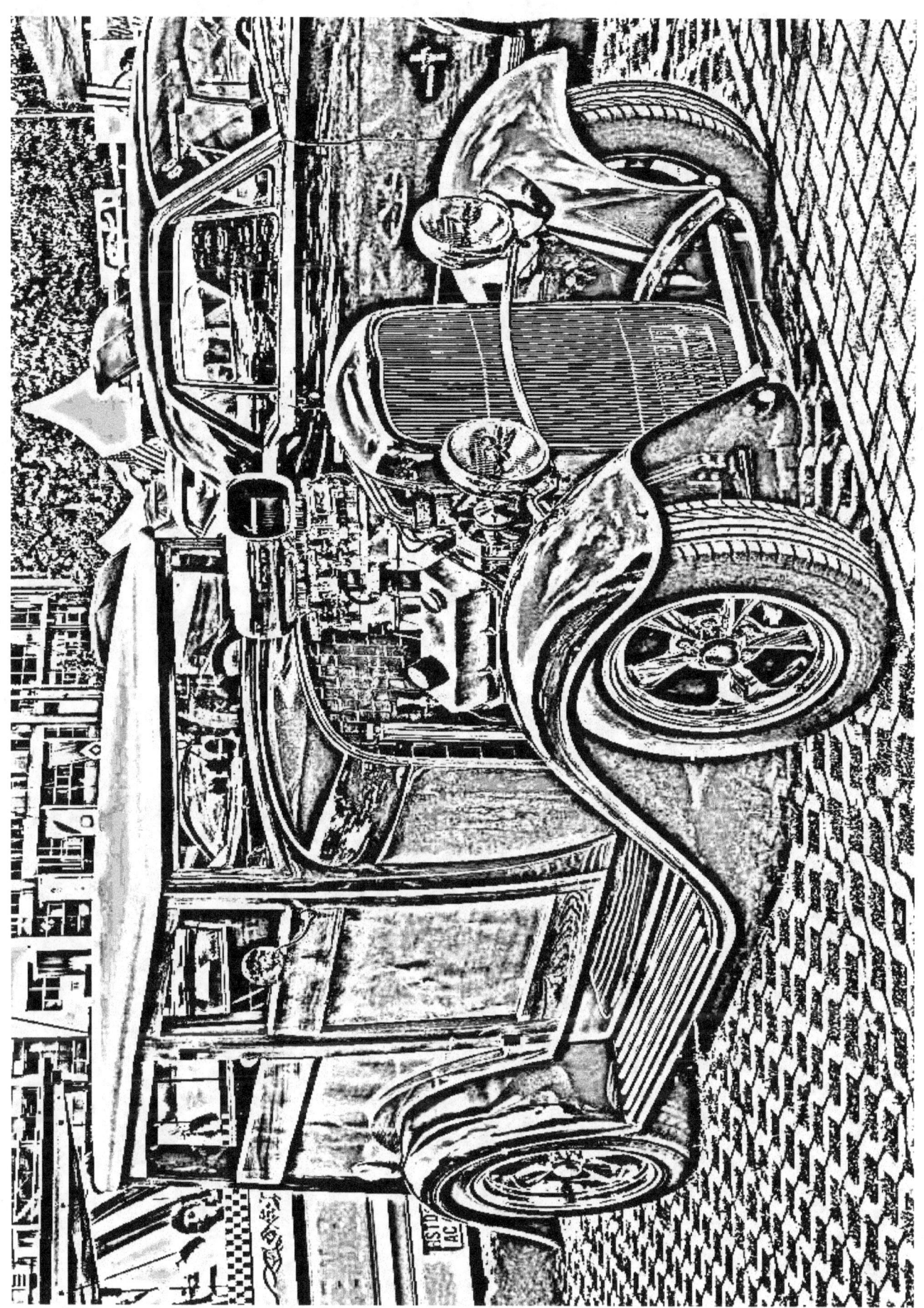

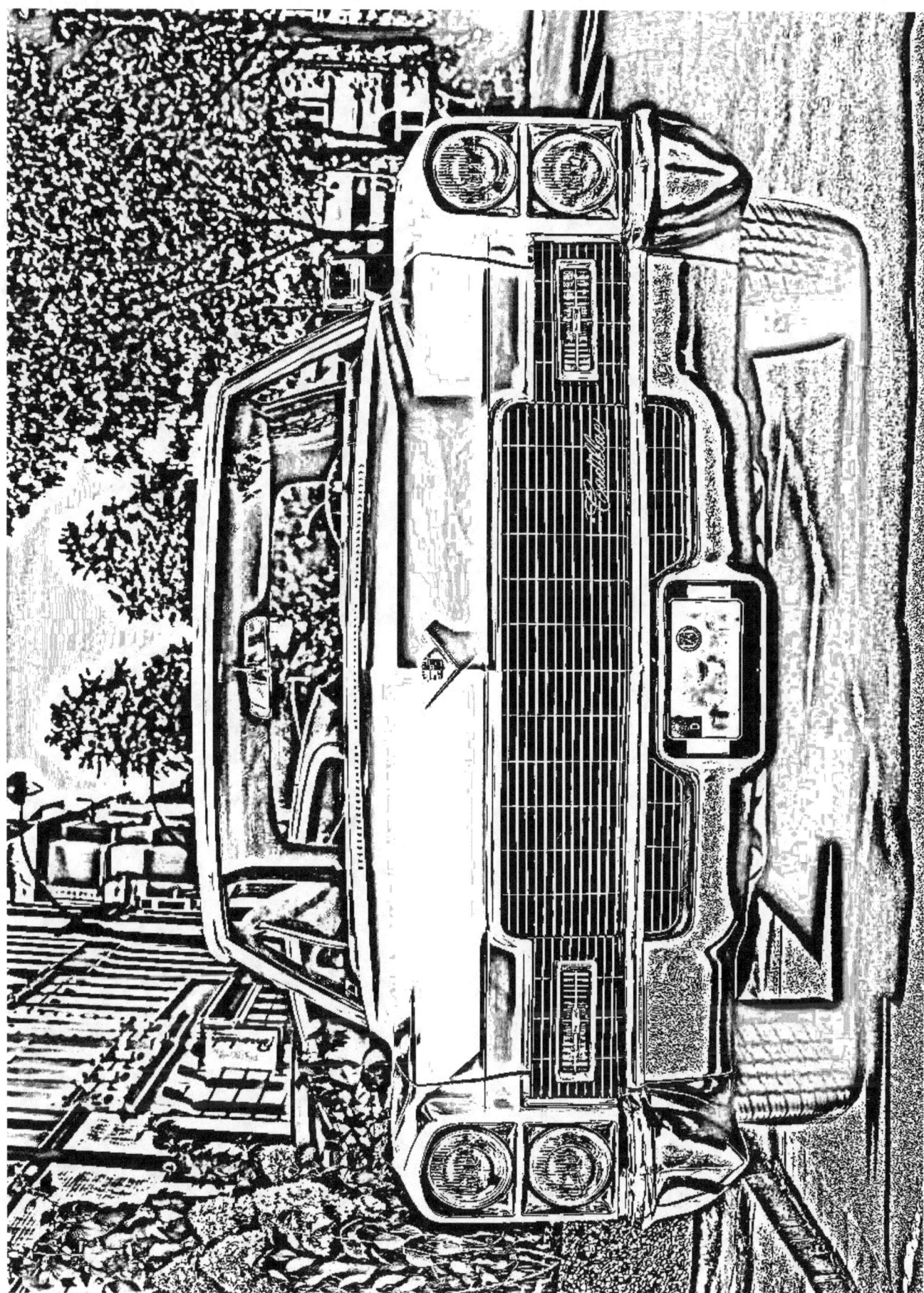

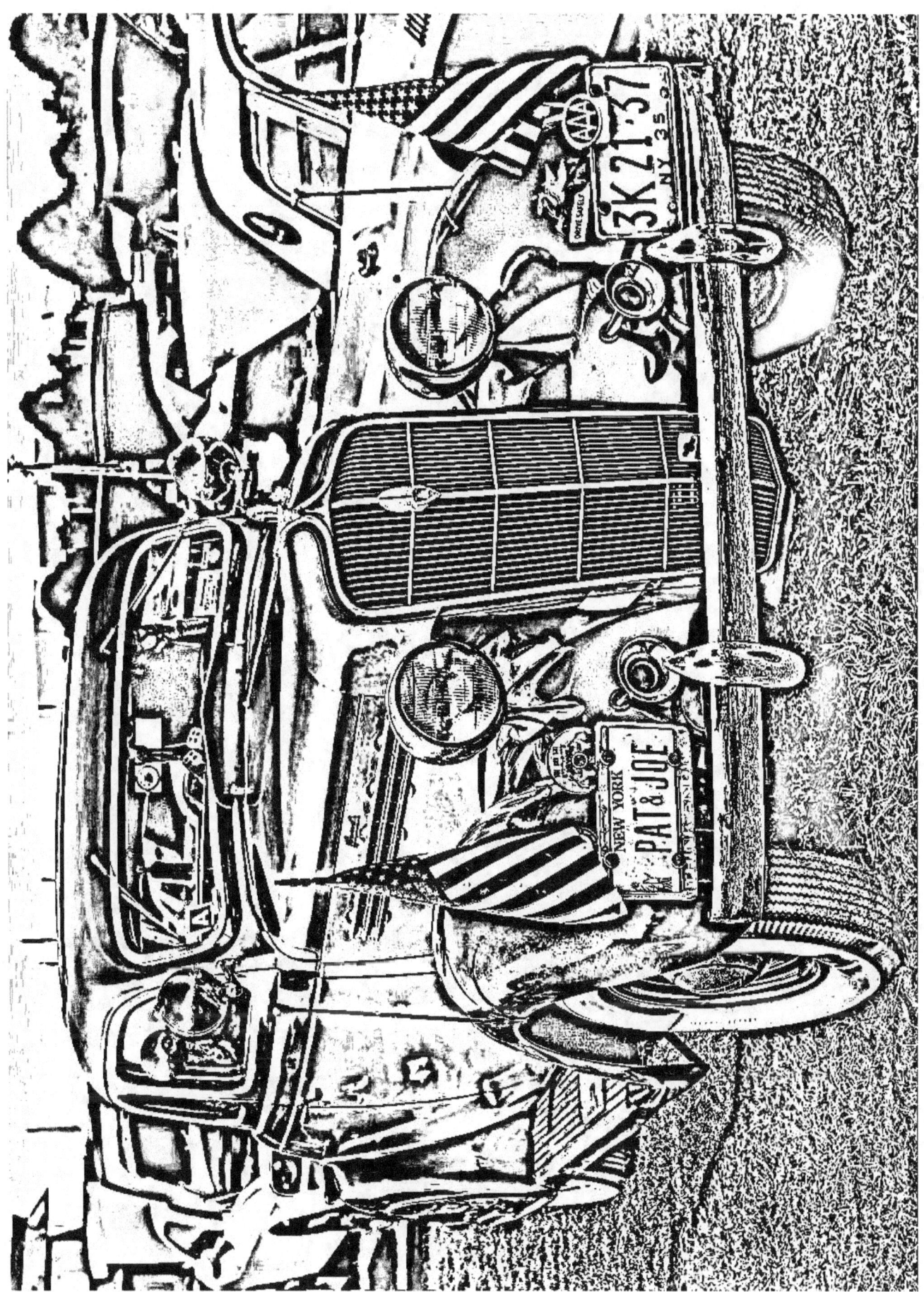

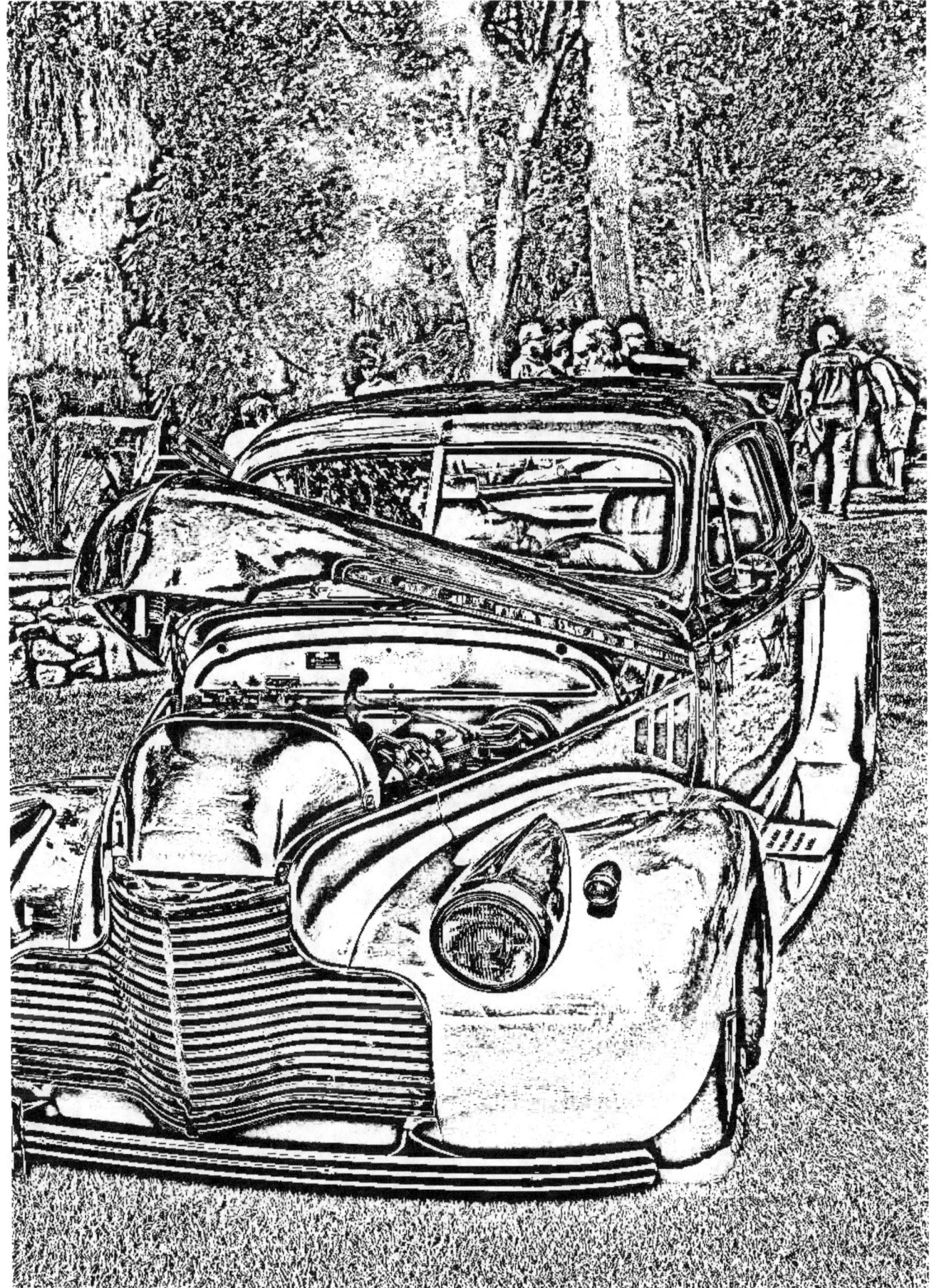

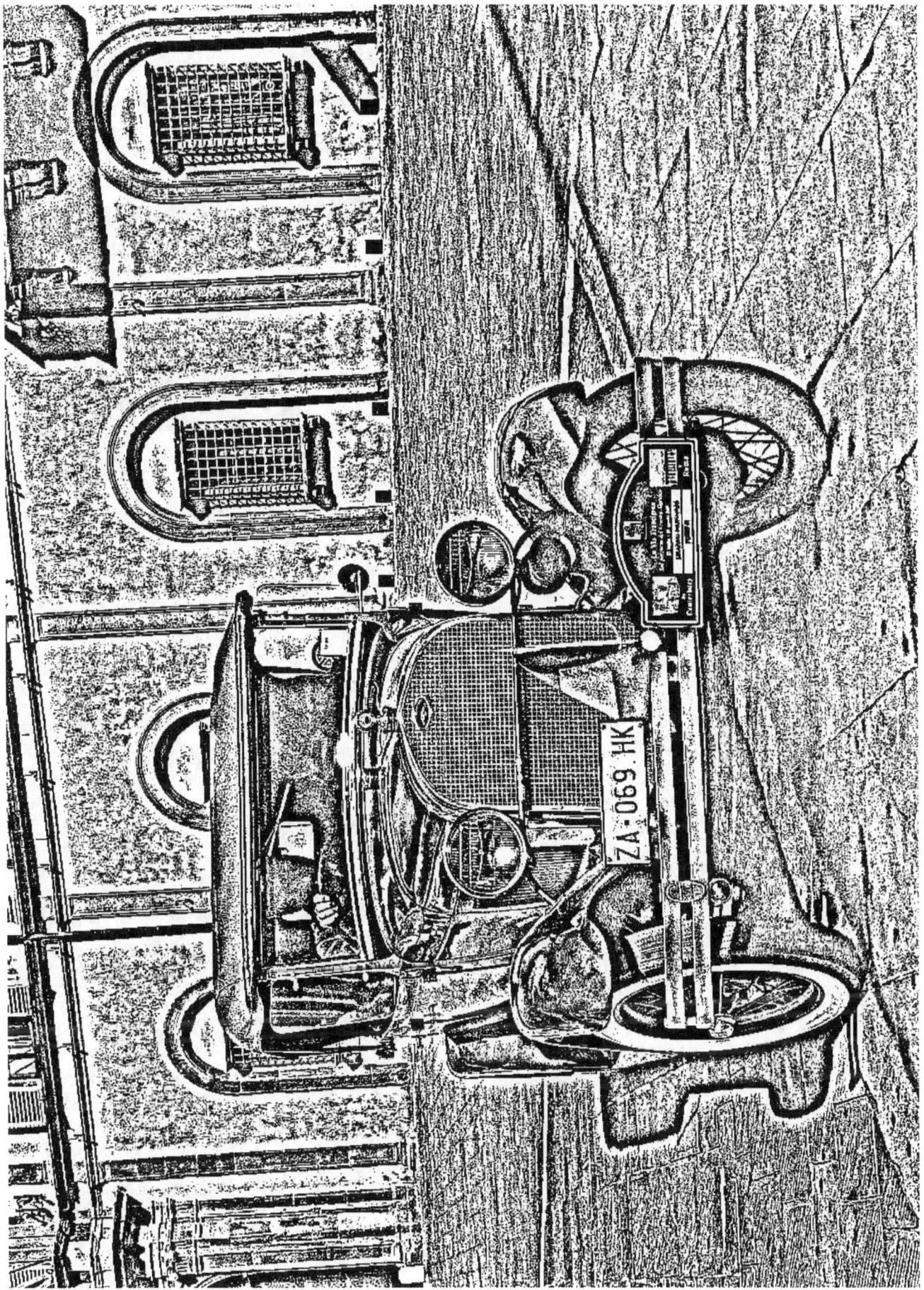

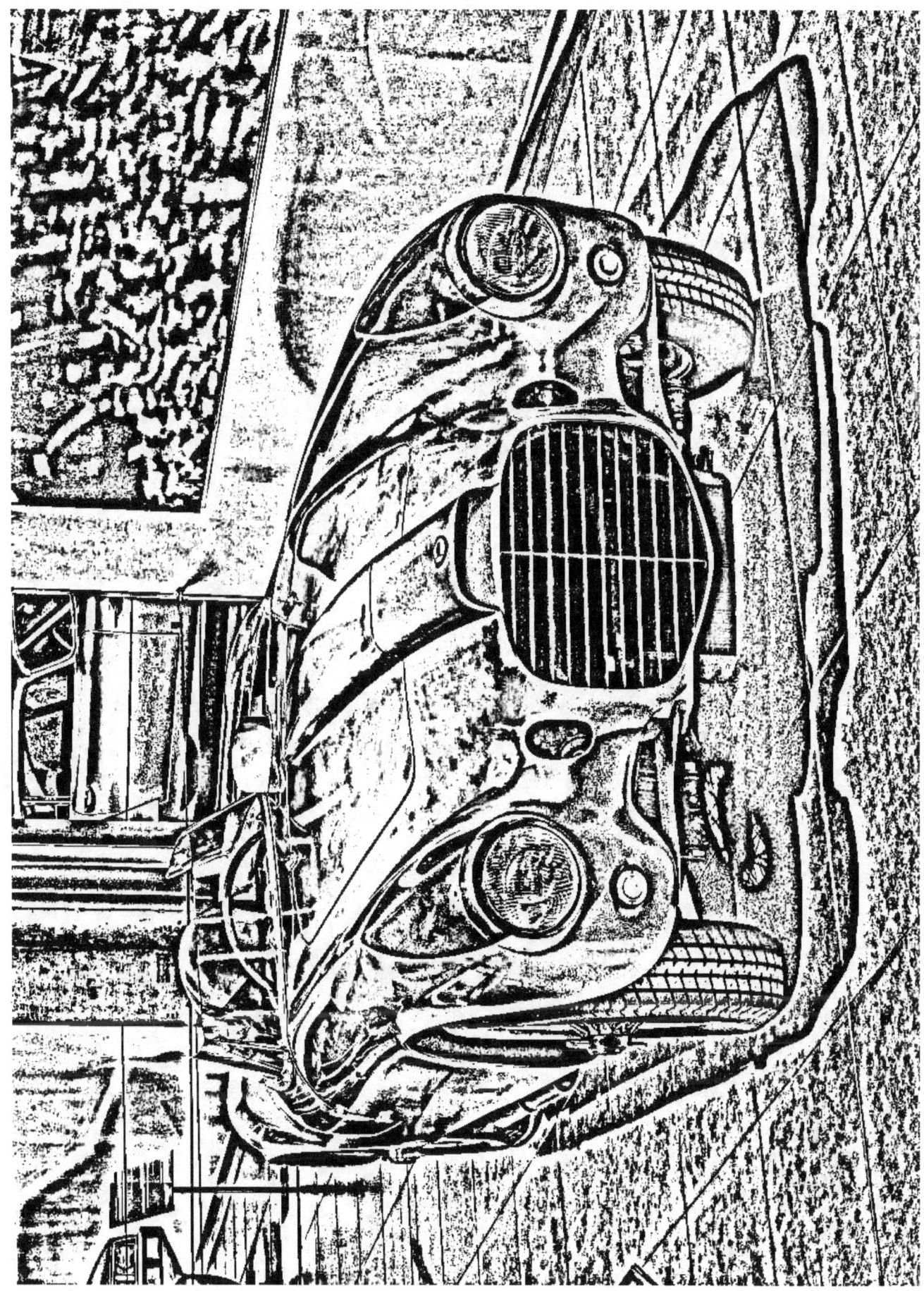

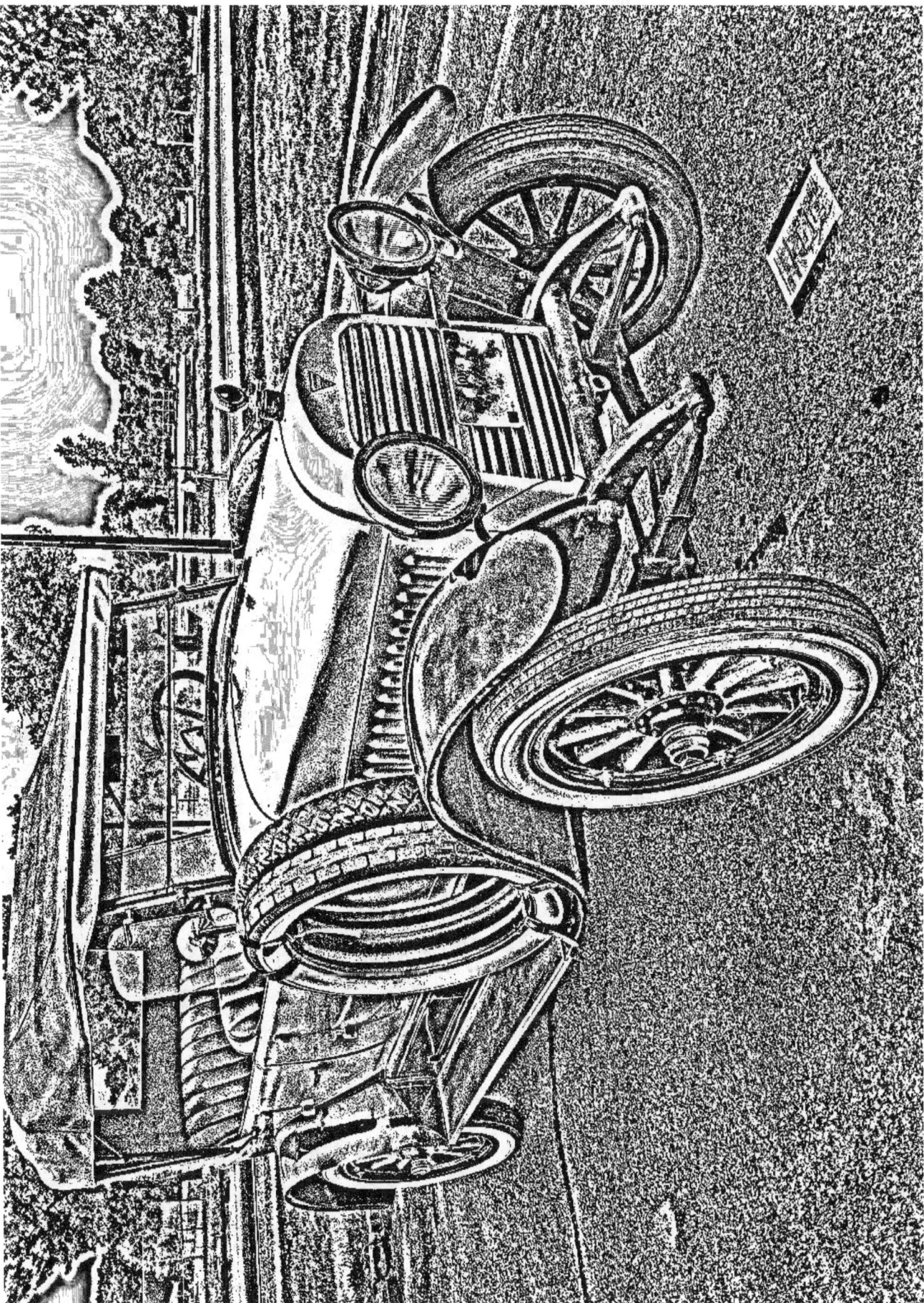

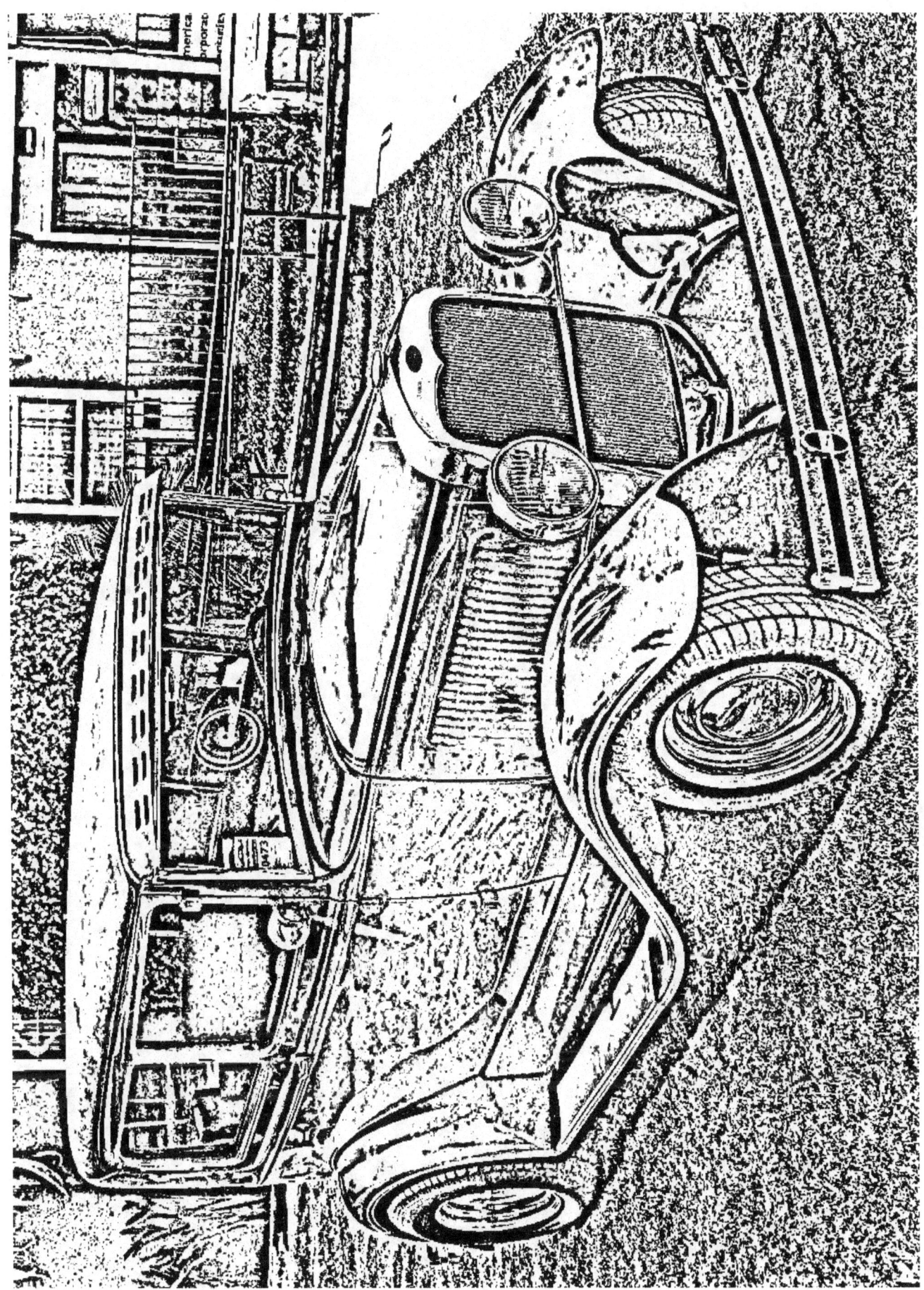

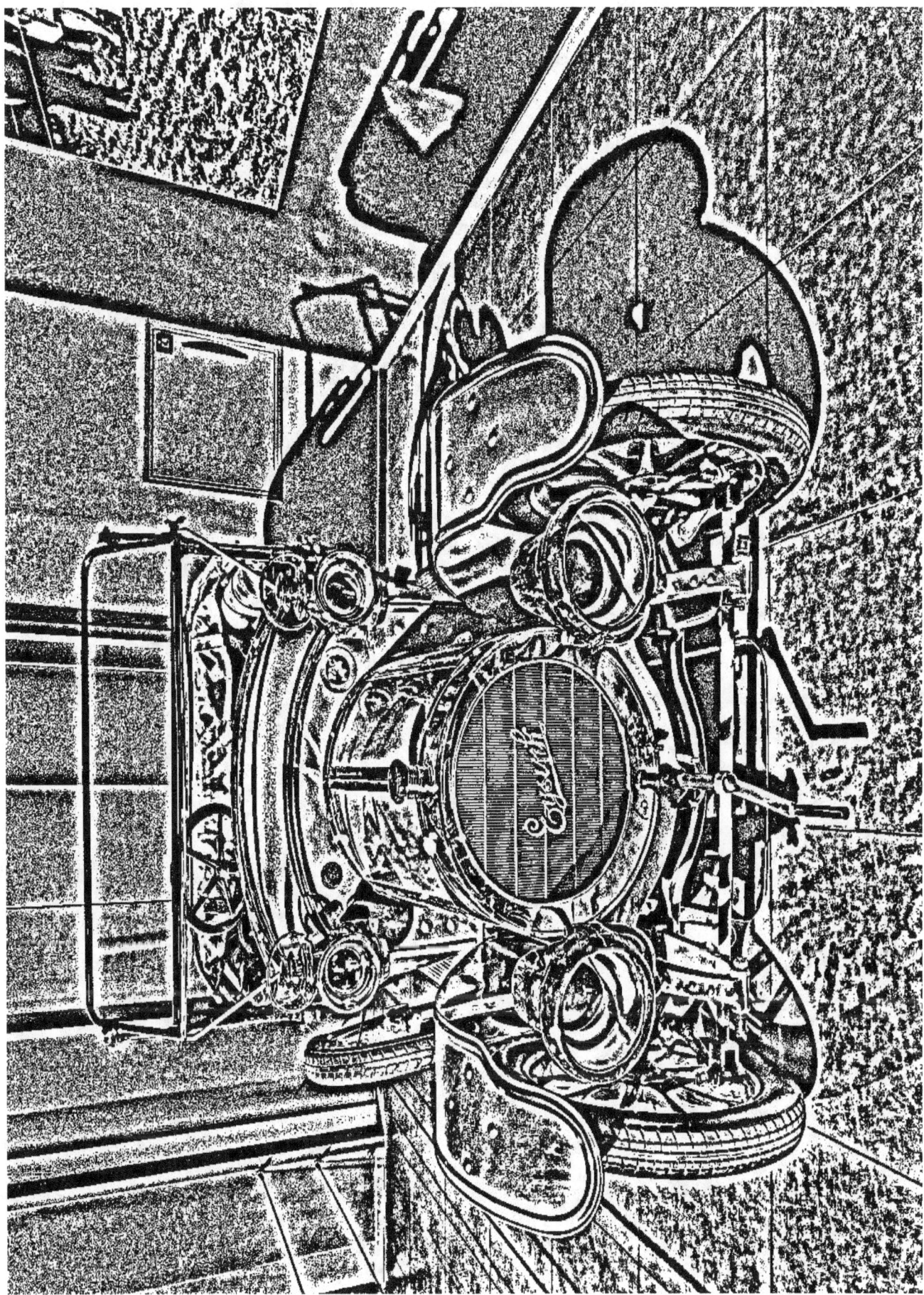

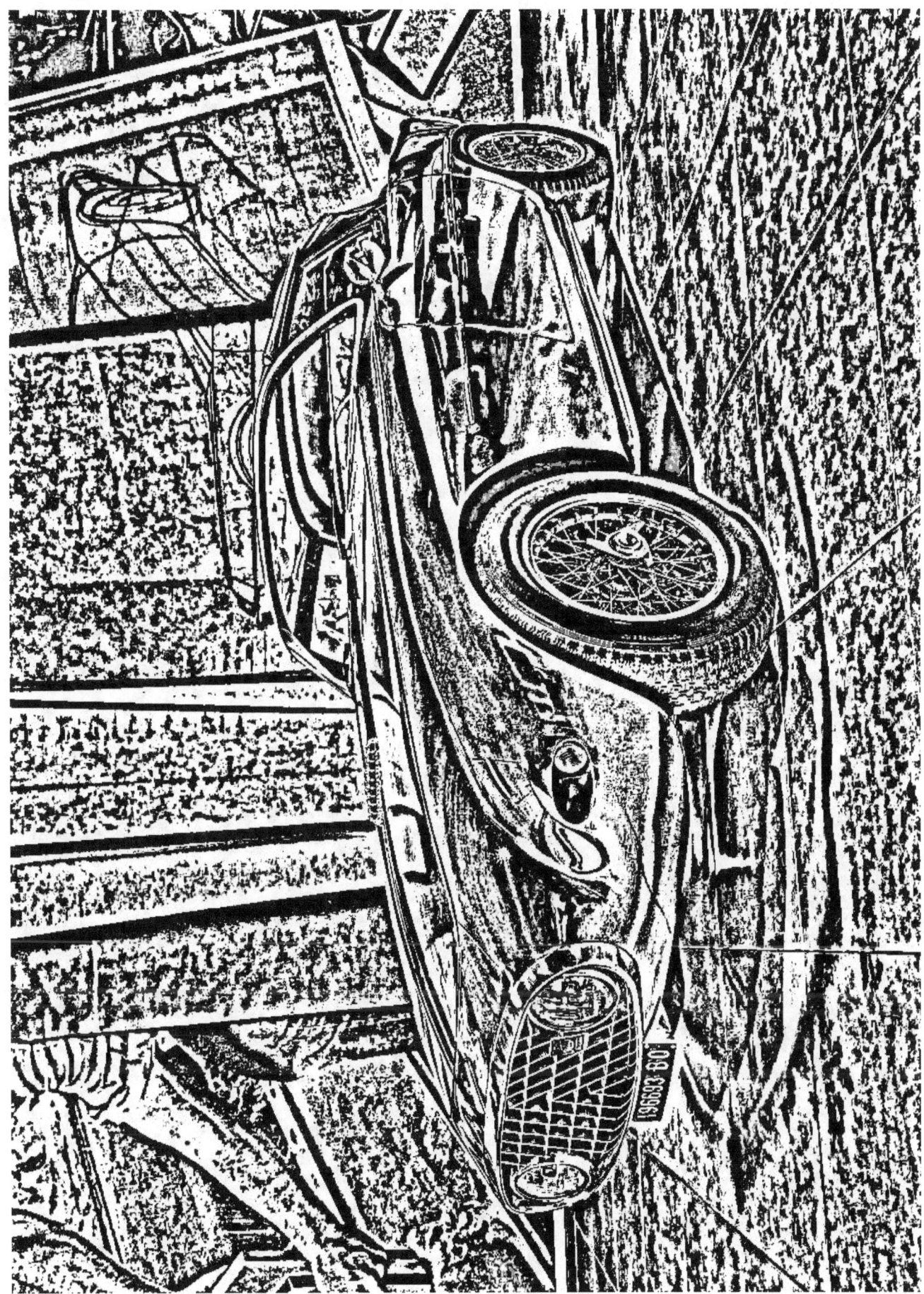

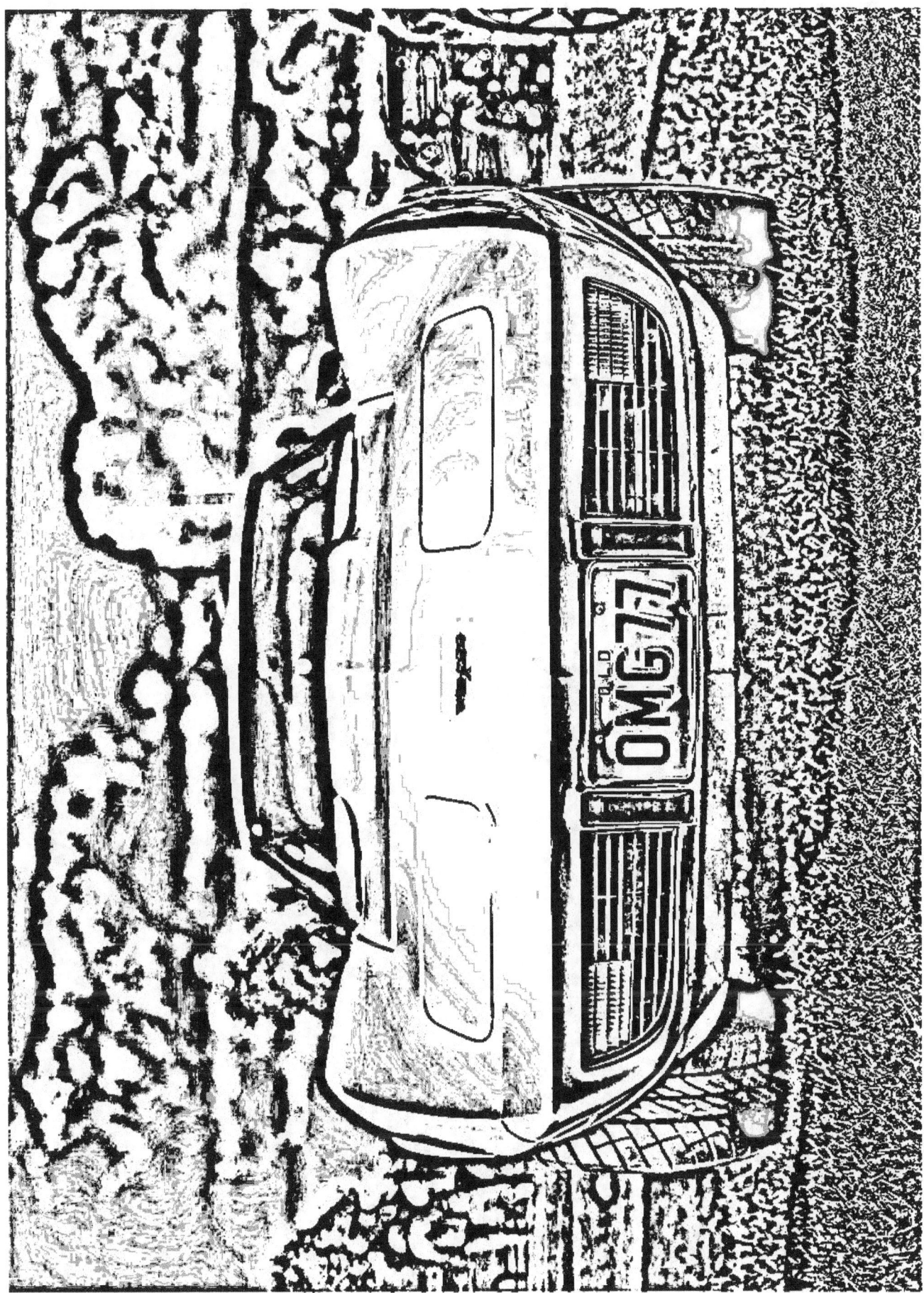

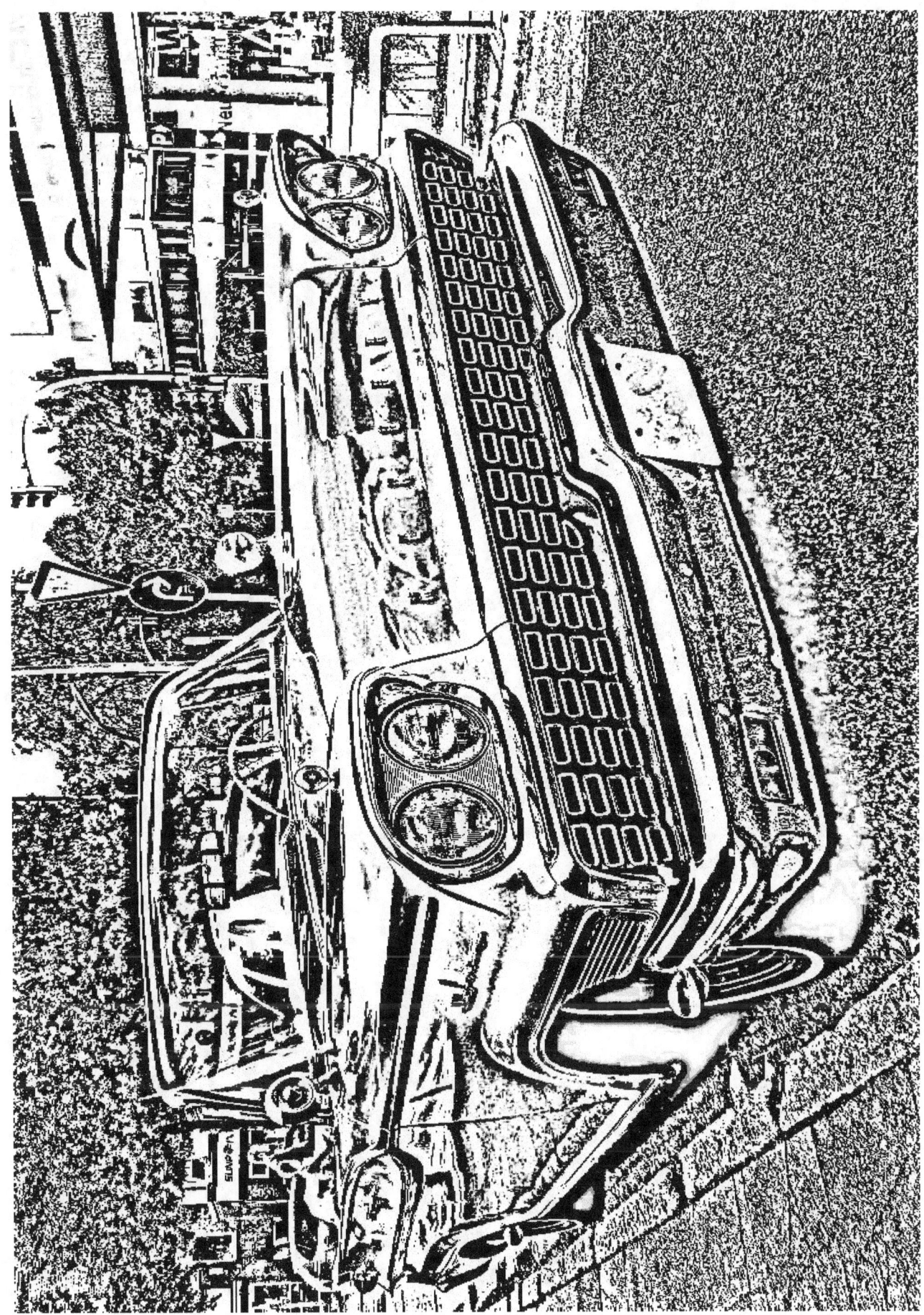

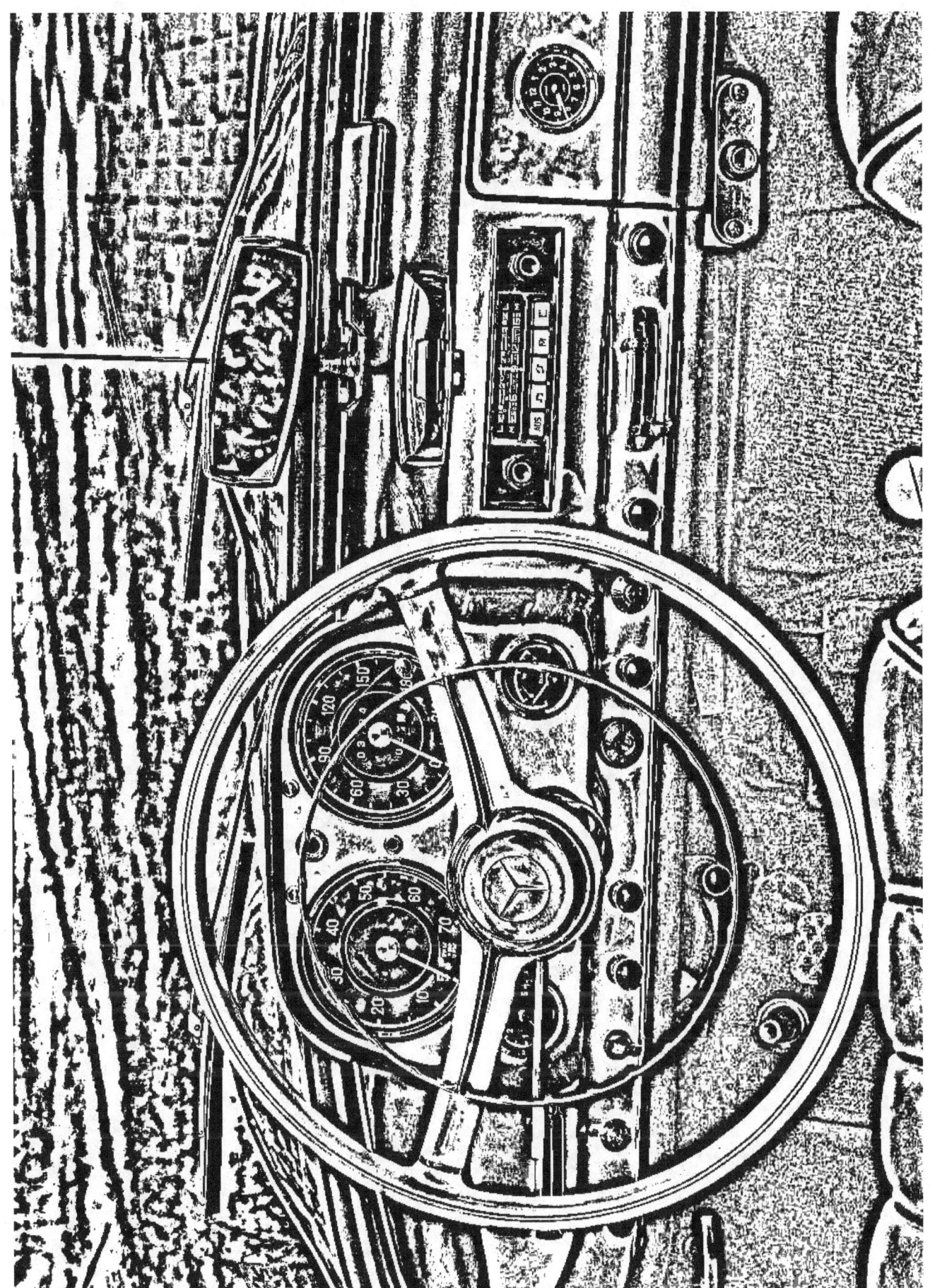

Thank you!
We hope you enjoyed our book.

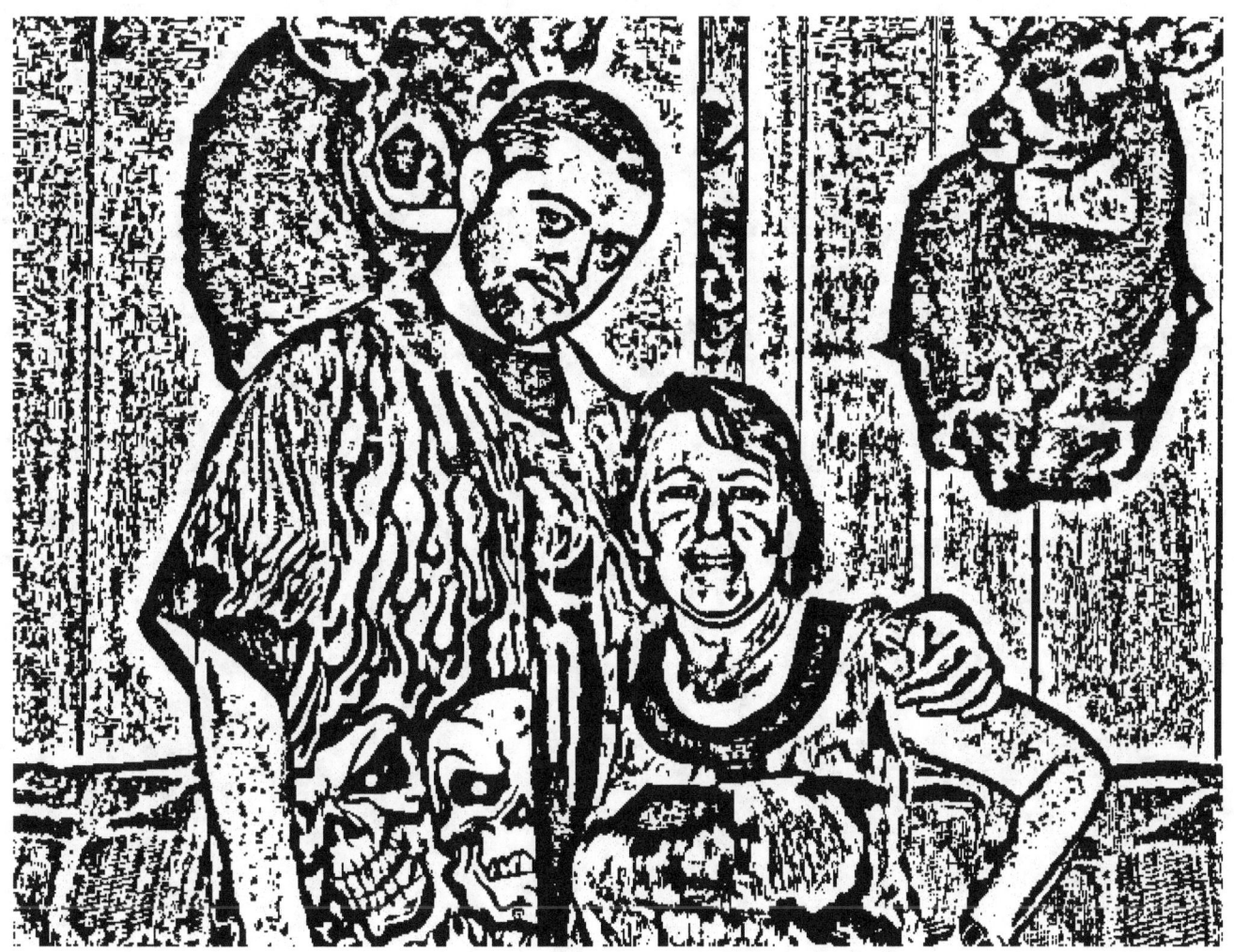

Watch for more color books by ARN Arts LLC.
Visit us at http://arnarts.wixsite.com/books